# The Farmer as Manager
*Wisdom from some I have known*

**Tony Giles,** OBE
Emeritus Professor of Farm Management
The University of Reading

ISBN: 1 872111 11 4

Published jointly by
The Institute of Agricultural Management

and

The Farm Management Unit,
The University of Reading

1996

Typeset and produced by Duce & Co, Reading. Telephone: (0118) 926 4805

# Contents

|   |   | Page |
|---|---|---|
| List of Illustrations … … … … … … … … … … … | | iv |
| Acknowledgements … … … … … … … … … … | | v |
| 1 | Writing this Book … … … … … … … … … | 1 |
| 2 | Not in my Wildest Dreams … … … … … … … | 5 |
| 3 | Entrée to the Farming Community … … … … … | 11 |
| 4 | Where and When … … … … … … … … … | 17 |
| 5 | How They Manage … … … … … … … … | 27 |
| 6 | What They Manage … … … … … … … … | 39 |
| 7 | No Man an Island … … … … … … … … | 53 |
| 8 | Cornerstones and Beliefs … … … … … … … | 61 |
| 9 | Just Like Christmas … … … … … … … … … | 73 |
| 10 | Stock Taking … … … … … … … … … … | 79 |
| Postscript … … … … … … … … … … … … | | 83 |

# List of Illustrations

1. String Diagrams at Bristol, mid 1950s
2. Extract from Farm Management Handbook, University of Bristol, 1955
3. First attendance at Oxford Farming Conference, 1960
4. First Overseas Farm Tour, Queensland, 1967
5. Another Oxford Farming Conference, 1975
6. Ex Chairmen of the FMA/CMA, 1982
7. The CMA Independence Working Party, 1987
8. Chairman and Secretary at the 1987 CMA Conference
9. FMU Study Tour to Wales, 1990
10. CMA National Farm Walk, Leckford Estate, 1990
11. At the 8th IFMA Congress, New Zealand, 1991
12. Presenting the Edith Mary Gayton Memorial Lecture, 1992
13. The E.M.G. audience
14. Off duty in Poland, 1992
15. At Churn Estates, 1993
16. Extract from Farm Business Data, The University of Reading, 1993
17. Retirement Party at Sonning Farm, 1993
18. Oilmen or farmers? Peter Cockburn on FMU Study Day, 1992
19. With CMA Chairman, John Carter, at 10th IFMA Congress
20. Author in retirement, 1995

The photograph on the cover, taken by Malcolm Stansfield, shows the author in conversation with two close friends and farm managers, Peter Cockburn (centre) and Andrew John (right), on the high part of Overbury Farms which the latter manages. The farms occupy a major part of Bredon Hill, a famous Cotswold outlier, from the highest point of which twelve of the old-styled counties can be seen. This photograph was taken on one of the annual 'private' farm visits referred to in Chapter 4 – Where and When.

# Acknowledgements

I cannot adequately say how grateful I have been over the years to all those – mentors, friends and colleagues – who, somewhere along the line, through schooldays, university and career, have helped, in various ways, to set me on, and keep me on, the path that provides the backcloth for this book.

I am, however, particularly grateful here to all those whom I have quoted, none of whose permission – believing they would not be offended by what I have ascribed to them – have I obtained!

If, between them, they have provided the gist of this book, others have helped, in different ways, to bring it physically into being. In order of their contributions, Jackie Reeves has word processed my scribbled manuscript into something that others could read and, despite her other work in my old Department, has kept pace with me throughout. Also despite her work, my wife, Heather, has, as usual, been prepared to listen to me read each chapter to her, hot off the 'press', combining her patience with her helpfully critical 'feel' for what I have been writing. Then there have been the photographers – professional and amateur, and finally, the combined professional skills of printers, Alan and Michael Duce, who have given the end product its attractive look.

I am grateful to them all, as I am to those in the Institute of Agricultural Management and Reading University's Farm Management Unit (notably Philip James and Malcolm Stansfield) who agreed to jointly finance and publish this volume.

A K Giles<br>
Spring 1996

*I am the farmer, stripped of love*
*and thought and grace by the land's harness;*
*But what I am saying over the fields'*
*Desolate acres, rough with dew,*
*Is, listen, listen, I am a man like you.*

R S Thomas

# 1 Writing This Book

The origins of this book go back a long way: to when I first embarked on the path to become an agricultural economist – in the University of Bristol in 1953. As a young Assistant Lecturer, spending much of my time out 'in the field' collecting financial data, I had the opportunity of getting to know, and listening to, a varied cross-section of West Country farmers and farm managers.

As experience would tell me, it is not only the best who disclose their business figures to relative strangers, but, even to my inexperienced eye at the time, it was clear to me that the best of those I was meeting – and of those I would be destined to meet in the future – were able managers; some of them outstandingly so, likely to be successful whatever their chosen industry. From the outset, long before they might have learnt anything useful from me, I began to learn from them: and have never stopped.

In particular, being a collector by nature, I began 'collecting' insightful and piquant statements that certain of the managers made about their personal management philosophies. Shaped in the hard school of practice, many of these statements would help to shape and confirm my own more theoretical views, influencing, over the years, what I have said in lectures and talks, and written in articles and books – especially this one.

The story of its origins now jumps a full quarter of a century, to 1979. In the intervening years I had remained committed to farm business management and continued to have close contact with farmers and farm managers. In 1960 I had moved to Reading University where I met a young farm manager who was in his first management job, on one of the University's farms. His name was Malcolm Stansfield, and despite the very different routes that our careers in farm management were to take in subsequent years – his in practical management on the University Farms and mine as an academic farm economist – our paths crossed frequently. We became increasingly aware that we were often thinking and saying the same kind of things about farm management and in 1979 our converging paths came together – leading indirectly to the writing of this present slim volume.

In that year, John Pearce retired from the University. For the previous thirty years his name had been synonymous with farm management at Reading. The reorganisation which followed his retirement, however, saw the formation of the University's Farm Management Unit which came about in the following way. Historically, farm management had been an important component in the wider interests of both the Department of Agriculture and the Department of Agricultural Economics and Management. In the interests of operational efficiency, however, the time had come to find an acceptable way of combining the farm management resources of both Departments, without weakening either's stake in the subject. In the event, the Farm Management Unit – bringing together colleagues from various parts of the University who had an interest in farm management, whilst leaving them as members of their respective parent Departments – was felt (and has proved) to be the best formula. It would be important, however, to the success of this arrangement that the Unit's two parent Departments (Agriculture and Agricultural Economics) should be directly involved in its leadership and, to this end, I was appointed (representing Agricultural Economics) as the Unit's first Director, with Malcolm Stansfield (having by now changed horses to become a full-time lecturer in the Department of Agriculture) as its Deputy Director.

In personal terms, this arrangement saw the start of a very special and enjoyable working relationship and close friendship, leading, within the space of two years, to the co-authorship of a book which embraced our combined views on farm management: *The Farmer as Manager*[1]. The split personality of the figure on the cover of the first edition – half businessman, half working farmer – was intended to reflect the dual role of the farmer as we saw it – 'the farmer as manager' no less – not, as many presumed, the two authors themselves! It was nevertheless the case that our differing backgrounds made the production of a joint text relatively straightforward, with my more theoretical introduction to each chapter followed by Malcolm Stansfield's practical illustrations.

We were at some pains in the first chapter to explain what the book was about and what it was *not* about. It was, we said 'about farming only in the sense that it is about the .... (overall) .... management of farms ... not about farm management in any narrow husbandry or financial accounting sense'. And while we hoped it would be of value to various groups of readers (e.g. students, advisers, bankers etc.) it was written essentially for those who actually managed farms. We stressed that we had tried to concern ourselves with those aspects of management which seemed to us to worry farm managers most and which they found most difficult to order in their minds.

Thus, while many books written by academics stem from their lecture notes, *The Farmer as Manager* was different, combining the structures of our professional training and experience with the informality and the insights we had both gained from countless conversations with farmers throughout Britain and abroad. Sometimes those conversations had been face to face with individuals, but very often with audiences at farmers' meetings,

---

[1] *The Farmer as Manager:* Tony Giles and Malcolm Stansfield. George Allen and Unwin, London 1980. Second Edition: CAB International, Wallingford, 1990.

conferences and discussion groups, in a wide variety of locations. Conscious, therefore, of the contribution that many practical farmers and farm managers had made (and continued to make) to the development of our own ideas, our book was dedicated:

> *"To all those who at one time or another have helped us to develop our views and who have encouraged us to write them down"*

That book was, nevertheless, a formal text, written by academics for practitioners; so by its very nature it could not be too informal, nor too anecdotal. Its purpose was to provide guidelines not answers, directions not decisions, frameworks of thinking, and I have little doubt that it was its degree of formality which left me with a lingering desire, that I have harboured ever since, to write the *other book*! The flip side, if you like; one that would be more anecdotal and personal, recalling some of the personalities who have influenced me, the various situations I have been in, and some of the statements that I have collected from those early days in the 1950s onwards – and which I have never stopped doing. So here, in the luxury of retirement, freed from academic niceties, I am writing it at last!

It has been helpful that I did not have to start with a blank sheet of paper. The *statements* and the *memories* were already there, on paper and in my mind; and, perhaps in anticipation, I used some of them in presenting (by way of a valedictory lecture) the Ninth Edith Mary Gayton Memorial Lecture in the University shortly before I retired[2]. To a considerable extent, that lecture has provided much of the framework and core material for this volume.

With Malcolm's permission (!) I decided to call it *The Manager as Farmer*. In the author's mind at least, that would provide a subtle contrast with The *Farmer as Manager*, encapturing some of the flavour of the changes that have occurred in the farming world during the years which have separated the two titles. In 1980 the general message carried by the *Farmer as Manager* was, simply, that survival and success depended on good management – and here were some guidelines. A decade and a half later, that message remains true, of course, but many of the newer generation of farmers and farm managers have been well trained at college and university in the theory of management, before going on to serve their managerial apprenticeships. Many of the businesses that they now manage, or help to manage, have become diversified in a wide variety of directions. During these years there has, I believe, been a levelling up of managerial ability in British farming and 'the managerial message' is now well understood. There are many good managers about (self employed and salaried) managing increasingly diverse

---

[2] Managing Now and the Lessons of Experience, in Management Matters in 1993. Farm Management Unit Study No 31, The University of Reading.

rural businesses: managers who, amongst other things, sometimes farm – *the manager as farmer* .

Finally, in this introductory chapter I should just add that the words in the sub-title – *some I have known* – imply, of course, that they have also known me. The circumstances of my earlier life which led me into the position where that has happened, and where a dialogue with the farming community has been possible, has never failed to surprise and amaze me. In the next chapter, therefore, I would like to explain how it came about.

# 2 Not in My Wildest Dreams

**EARLY YEARS**
Born in 1928 in Rochester, Kent, on the east bank of the Medway, I was a Man of Kent – just; unlike the upstarts on the other side of the river: London overspill and, therefore, Kentish Men, not Men of Kent – an important distinction!

My boyhood home was some two miles away from the river on the chalk slopes leading southwards to the North Downs: or, as I well remember my school geography master saying 'on the dip slope of a denuded anticline – but it's quite safe!'. When I was aged about twelve, at the height of the Battle of Britain, I had my first occasion to get acquainted with the resistant properties of chalk as I helped to dig a six feet deep hole in the garden to accommodate an Anderson air-raid shelter. I did not, of course, know then that I was destined to live the greater part of my life close to chalk – as well as to use it on blackboards!

Essentially a 'townie' *(then* and *now)* there was nothing in my early boyhood to suggest that I was heading for a career that would in any way be associated with farming – or, for that matter, with teaching. Not evacuated ('If we're going to go' my mother said, 'we'll all go together' – a sentiment with which I hardly agreed!), and with schooling severely curtailed in the early years of the war, I had a grandstand view of the war in the air, so that aviation, followed closely by sport, were my chief spare-time interests – as they still tend to be.

It is true that my maternal grandparents (who ran a horse and cab business in Gillingham) had sent their only son, Sidney, to be a farm pupil (as apprentices were called in those days) in Leicestershire, and had bought a small farm a few miles out of Rochester for him to return to after the Great War. Sadly he did not return and the farm was sold. That, of course, was a long time before I had even been thought about, but my mother talked a lot about her brother (to whom I was often likened) and the farm. Fascinated by the tales about him, it was many years later (in 1967), when on my way to give a lecture at Brooksby Agricultural College, that I made the effort to locate the farm, in the nearby village of Woodhouse Eaves, where the young Sidney Kent had been a pupil before going to France in 1914. I met several members of the family who employed him, including one elderly daughter who remembered him well; his girlfriend, I suspected.[3]

---

[3] I have written separately about this for family consumption: *Sidney George Kent at Woodhouse Eaves.*

It is also true that my own father, returning from the Great War, set up (with the help of a bicycle) his own small business selling confectionery into retail shops – a venture which slowly developed into a substantial wholesale grocery business which still exists at the time of writing.

Run by my brother and sister, it is the only remaining business of its kind in Kent. It flourished perhaps most in the years immediately after the Second World War, as food rationing slowly ended and before supermarkets and modern packaging put many traditional corner shops – the bulk of my father's clientele – out of business. In those days, however, many basic groceries – fats, cheese, sugar, dried fruit and various cereals, for example – were supplied to wholesalers in bulk, to which they 'added value' (no new concept!) by 'decanting' into the very much smaller packaging required for retail sale (eg 1lb). There was, therefore, plenty of pocket money to be earned by an under-employed schoolboy, and I became very familiar with small blue bags and greaseproof paper – and have been a good 'wrapper' ever since!

I cannot, of course, know how far either of these experiences – my fascination with a would-be uncle who, but for war, would have farmed, and my more practical involvement at the other end of what we would now refer to as the food-chain – had any sub-conscious effect on my eventual choice of career. But I cannot recollect any recognisable ambition to go in either of these directions and believe it would be stretching the imagination to suggest otherwise. I was to remain undecided about a career until well into my twenties, at which point I was happy to leave my brother and elder sister to the hard work of running a family business.

Something, however, that I also recall from boyhood – and which I believe may have indirectly influenced my choice of career more than anything else – was my fascination (in *total* contrast to my own children and step children years later!) at looking out of the car window at *whatever* there was to see. In the immediate post war years, the novelty of a family car had not finally worn off and, indeed, may have been rekindled as petrol was de-rationed. So it was still the fashion for the family to be taken out for a 'run' in the car. On these occasions (when I couldn't wriggle out of them) my eyes would be glued to the window, fascinated by the geography of the landscape – whether natural or man-made. It was a fascination that I have never lost: wanting to know where I am, what I am looking at and why it looks as it does.

## EDUCATION

This interest in topography was fed when, in 1944, putting off the necessity to get a job and, armed with a 'doodlebug matric'[4], I proceeded into the

---

[4] Because examinations were frequently interrupted by VI raids (Doodlebugs) we believed at the time that examiners were accordingly lenient hence the phrase 'doodlebug matric'.

sixth form to take arts subjects, including geography. In due course, success at that level opened the door to university, which I had not previously contemplated. Still without any career preferences and anxious, therefore, to keep my options open, I responded to the advice of the school careers master who suggested that 'If you don't know what you want to do, economics is a good idea'!

Progress in that direction was to be interrupted, however, by two years of National Service which, like many, I have valued more in retrospect than I did at the time. My interest in aircraft made the RAF a natural choice although in the two years I seldom came near a plane! But, despite my general aversion to service life, I had a 'good' national service by any standards. Disproving the belief that they usually managed to put round pegs into square holes, the RAF trained me in the arts of aptitude testing, gave me a Commission and stationed me in the Air Ministry which was then in the centre of London, at Aldwych. Part of my job was to travel to universities throughout the United Kingdom testing undergraduates who wished to join their university's Air Squadron. It was all very useful, helping me to make my own choice of university – The Queen's University of Belfast – and developing skills, including statistics, that would be professionally valuable later on.

Apart from the fact that I had been offered a place there, and had been impressed by its friendliness on several RAF visits, I chose Queen's for two other reasons that were important to me at the time: first, because it was far enough away to discourage me from popping home in term time; and secondly for the quality of its rugby. The nucleus of the Irish national team was in residence there at the time and I was keen to try my luck in good company – and was not disappointed.

I should perhaps add here that I have been saddened, in recent times, to see university campuses regularly empty out from about mid-day on Friday until Monday morning, with many undergraduates spending time and money elsewhere, denying themselves many of the pleasures of university life. I must also say, remembering my own experience, that I have always had sympathy for students who have chosen their university on other than purely academic grounds: like the student, keen on horse-racing, who told me that he chose Reading because it was half way between Newbury and Ascot!

In due course, my economics degree was to further feed my interest in the countryside in a way that I did not anticipate. The course included large segments of economic history (much of which, almost by definition, has a rural basis) and economic geography (much of which is based on land-use and other natural resources), and slowly these subjects began to blend together for me, and mature into a genuine interest in the landscape – in what mankind does to and with it.

## DAY OF RECKONING

As graduation approached in 1953, and the pressure to think seriously about a career could not be avoided any longer, the desire to combine some aspects of my economics training with the broad interest in land-use that had been gestating for a decade or more, pointed me towards agricultural economics. An article which appeared at the time in the Sunday Times, describing the management accounting techniques used by the well known Hampshire farmer, Rex Paterson – pioneer of low cost milk production, whom I was later to know well – further sharpened my mind and encouraged me to apply for one of *four* vacancies for Assistant Agricultural Economists at the University of Bristol. There were very few ready trained agricultural economists in those days. Entrants into the profession were a mixed bag, but mostly with a degree either in agriculture or economics: each group picking up, during their employment, the part of the subject they lacked – a more difficult and lengthy process, I subsequently discovered, for the economist than the agriculturist.

With farming, however, beginning to face its post-war difficulties, the 1950s were an expansionist time for agricultural economics, which, much more than now, was, in those days, very farm oriented. This was reflected by the four new vacancies at Bristol which suggested better than usual odds for an applicant. Even so, I felt fortunate to be appointed having decided to reply 'Nothing' to the chairman's opening question: 'How much do you know about agriculture other than ploughing up rugby pitches?' It was not the first time that I was wise not to feign technical knowledge that I did not possess, soon learning that there are few groups of people who are quicker to sniff out the bogus than farmers.

When the time came to leave Northern Ireland I did so with a mixture of emotions, having hugely enjoyed my four years in the Province: a more peaceful place then than it subsequently became. My initial impressions about the friendliness of Queen's had not been wrong and I had felt very much at home in the invigorating, no-nonsense city of Belfast. I left behind many friends and good memories but took with me my degree (in those days more of a passport to employment than more recently) a rugby blue and a prospective wife – and headed with enthusiasm for Bristol.

Looking back on my life up to that date I was aware (and have been increasingly so ever since) of the important part played by chance, and by the many individuals and organisations to whom one has cause to be grateful in various ways. In my case, this included my parents who (unlike many) put no pressure on me whatsoever to make what might have been premature career decisions (although goodness knows what they were thinking and saying in private!); those few school teachers who inspired, including the careers master whose almost 'throw away' advice had set me on the economics path; a fellow student (later to become a Deputy Vice

Chancellor) who drew my attention to Bristol University's job advertisement; the RAF, of more value than I realised at the time; and those at Bristol (and later Reading) who gave me jobs and who helped me in ways that I could not have known earlier – *not in my wildest dreams* – would lead to a career in which I have had the luxury of combining my professional enthusiasm for *management* (the empirical arm of economics that always interested me most) with a more gradually cultivated fascination in the shaping of landscape.

In the process I have had the additional pleasure of getting to know, and learning from, many farmers and farm managers, including some who are now close personal friends. Not in my wildest dreams ...............

# 3 Entree to the Farming Community

**BRISTOL**
This Chapter continues in autobiographical vein. Unlike many post-war farm economists who moved sideways into other aspects of agricultural economics – *policy* and *development* were the favourites – I started and was destined to stay with farm management throughout. Even the second strings that I developed to my bow in mid-career (the rural-urban interface) and towards the end (the history of agricultural economics) were not divorced from *farm management*, which remained my central professional interest over a forty-year career[5].

Geographically speaking, those forty years were divided between the first six spent in the University of Bristol, followed by a much longer thirty-four at Reading. Although in university employment throughout, at no stage did I feel in any sort of ivory tower: the 'applied' nature of farm management as a subject – not to mention 'practising what I preached' within the increasingly constrained circumstances of the university world – made no room for any such feelings.

In terms of what I was actually *doing* in the world of farm management, however, I have differentiated, in my own mind, between the 'liaison' years (from the beginning until about 1970) and the more 'academic' years from then until retirement. In a sense they were all *academic* years, with no hard and fast divide; but there was a gradual change of emphasis towards more academic activities which, nevertheless, allowed me to remain in close contact with farmers and farm managers. Let me explain.

Without a significant teaching role, Bristol University's Department of Agricultural Economics was destined to be wound up following a 'rationalisation' exercise within the subject in the early 1970s. When I joined it, however, in 1953, it was one of ten Provincial centres, all based in universities or colleges, which collectively formed the Provincial Agricultural Economics Service (PAES). Set up in 1945, this service was responsible, amongst other things, for its share of the Farm Management Survey (the FMS, but now the Farm Business Survey, FBS) and closely related enterprise costs. Previously, these centres had been part of a wider

---

[5] In this respect I was like my opposite number at Wye College, and close friend, John Nix. Both from urban backgrounds and both pure economists by training, we occupied the only two Chairs in orthodox farm management to have existed in the UK, and have both remained committed to the subject, even after retirement.

pre-war Provincial Agricultural Advisory Service (also based in universities and colleges) out of which the National Agricultural Advisory Service (NAAS) was to emerge in 1946. In this post-war reorganisation, it was decided, however, that economists, because of the particular nature of their work, which required visible evidence of independence from Government, should be left in the universities – clearly separated from the Government's newly formed advisory service, but with which, for the next two or three decades, there was going to be close 'liaison'[6].

It was inevitable that, initially, NAAS would be staffed largely by husbandry specialists trained in the pre-war and wartime years. Generally speaking, therefore, they had little or no acquaintance with questions of financial management and, for this reason, were ill-equipped to cope with the growing demand for financial advice that was beginning to emanate from a peacetime farming in which 'production at all costs' was no longer the main objective. Something needed to be done to cope with this situation and, rather than fill the gap by immediately appointing farm management specialists within the ranks of NAAS (which at the time could have been difficult), it was decided to appoint Farm Management Liaison Officers (FMLOs) at each of the PAES centres. With the backing of their established departments, these FMLOs were to be responsible for training and working with NAAS staff until the Advisory Service became self sufficient in giving farm management advice. In the event, and perhaps not surprisingly, that self sufficiency was achieved only quite slowly and at a varying pace around the country, so that FMLOs were to remain involved with NAAS up to the time that it became ADAS (The Agricultural Development and Advisory Service) in 1971. By then, the Service had 'grown' its own Regional Farm Management Specialists, each leading a management team, and FMLOs (their job done) were largely able to withdraw into more orthodox academic existences[7].

Arriving on to this scene in Bristol, in 1953, as a raw economics graduate with no knowledge of agriculture at all, I was fortunate in a number of ways. First (presumably *because* of my economics background) I was assigned as the Assistant to Bristol's Farm Management Liaison Officer, who was heavily involved in the early throes of indoctrinating NAAS advisers in the arts of

---

[6] Initially the PAES had its own conditions of employment, separate from those of the universities in which it was lodged, until it was 'assimilated' in 1956, and then fully 'integrated' into universities in 1968 at which point the PAES, as such, ceased to exist and the work continued in orthodox university departments. (The Provincial Agricultural Economics Service 1945-1968. Its Origins, Form, Demise and Legacy. A K Giles, Occasional Paper No 1, Department of Agricultural Economics and Management, The University of Reading 1993.)

[7] Farm Management Liaison: A Unique Era. A K Giles with P J James. Study No 32, The Farm Management Unit, The University of Reading, 1993.

financial analysis and planning. Secondly, the FMLO in question was Stuart Wragg, first and foremost an economist who, despite a diffident 'platform' manner, had the ability to engage those – farmers and their advisers alike – who were prepared to listen to him. At the time, it did not include everyone.

Amongst those, however, who *were* ready to listen, were an unusually enthusiastic advisory staff in the County of Gloucestershire. On Bristol's doorstep and led by the legendary 'W E' Jones (later Sir Emrys and Director of the Service) it would be no exaggeration to say that 'W E' and his colleagues – who included such farm management enthusiasts as Derek (later Lord) Barber, Jim Butt-Evans, Eric Carter and later Philip Bolam – became 'disciples' of Wragg, and (notwithstanding the early influence of Blagburn at Reading and Wallace at Cambridge) the County Headquarters at Elmbridge Court became the 'cradle' of farm management advisory work in this country. Although personally feeling quite overawed on my first visit there (as a week-old 'agricultural economist'!) I was fortunate to continue to go there regularly and to cut my professional teeth in such company – amongst whom I have had lasting friendships.

My *entrée to the farming community* had now begun. Initially travelling with Stuart Wragg whose way of thinking did much to influence my own – I was privileged to meet some of the leading farmers in the counties surrounding Bristol. Notable amongst them were Wiltshire's Wilfred Cave – pioneer producer of milk and corn on the chalk downs; Ted Owens – intensive grassland farmer in Somerset with strong views about opportunities for youth and training; and Oscar Colburn – the genteel Cotswold sheep breeder, and member of the Cygnets, – a highly select farmer discussion group based on The Swan Hotel in Bibury and all of whom I was to meet[8].

At this stage, most of my personal contribution to the liaison work consisted of preparing data handbooks (based on the FMS) for use in comparative analysis: a task which in one capacity or another was to stay with me for the whole of my career. This was a desk job, but, after a short training in Work-Study techniques – all the vogue in the late 'fifties and early 'sixties – I escaped into the 'field', armed with a stop watch, to advise on some of farming's more repetitive routines such as milking, egg packing and cheese making. Rising at 4 am in order to be on farms in time to record the morning milking is indelibly imprinted on my memory – and I still have some string-diagrams to prove it!

---

[8] The six farmer members of this group were, alphabetically, Oscar Colburn, Robert Henly, Philip Hough, Maurice Lait, Tony Morris and Derek Pearce. Joined by Stuart Wragg (Bristol University) and Emrys Jones and Derek Barber (NAAS Gloucester) the genesis of the group had initially been in comparing their farm accounts, but its activities developed to include visiting speakers and visits outside the county. Derek Pearce (in 1958) and Oscar Colburn (in 1989) became farmer authors, both of whom I have quoted elsewhere in the book.

In addition to my modest contribution to the Department's advisory work, I was required to take a share in the routine collection of FBS accounts and similar data – work which is now carried out by professional Investigational Officers, but who had not been invented at the time. Having been instructed in the mysteries of farm accounts, and taught to drive the departmental car (salaries at the time did not permit ownership!) I can still remember the day that I set off alone in a car, for the first time, to collect my first account in the uplands of Herefordshire – and can recall few more stressful days in my entire career. My first experience of public speaking was hardly worse!

In theory, all of this 'required' work was supposed to occupy no more than half of the available time, with the other half available for personal research. I needed no encouragement to embark down that route and, anxious not to be exposed by my non-agricultural background, concentrated initially on labour relations in the industry. Teaming up with an Aberdonian colleague, Bill Cowie[9], we embarked on a series of studies together, examining, in turn, reasons for the 'drift from the land', the 'tied cottage controversy' and, after we had both left Bristol, a broader examination of 'the training, pay and status' of farm workers. Very different from each other in personality and temperament, we worked well together and each study involved us in talking both to farmers – and their workers – some of whom are quoted later on.

## READING

My six years in Bristol had served as a valuable apprenticeship, mainly under the watchful eye of Stuart Wragg. He had steered the middle course of sheltering me when the going was likely to be too rough (as it could be in those days) and occasionally throwing me into deep but calm water. As a result I was confident enough to apply for (and obtain) the FMLO's post at Reading University caused by the early retirement of Paddy Blagburn, the first FMLO to have been appointed, and famous in farm management circles for his *System and Yield Indexes*. I was leaving behind one master of his trade to follow in the footsteps of another, and I did so now with a wife, two children and a car – and, incidentally, happy memories of playing rugby for Clifton where I also met farmers!

Close liaison was to continue between the National Agricultural Advisory Service and University departments of Agricultural Economics for another decade after I joined Reading. Now, however, I was in the front line and spent most of that decade busily engaged in training and working with advisers in the field; at times feeling more like a 'rep' than an academic, criss-crossing Central Southern England day after day. There was close liaison also with other FMLOs, especially at Wye College (with whom

---

[9] Soon after I left Bristol for Reading, W J G (Bill) Cowie left for Newcastle university, where he became a senior lecturer, before a sadly premature death.

Reading shared a MAFF Region), first with Ian Reid, and then with his successor, John Nix, with whom I have enjoyed a close working and personal relationship ever since. I also continued to collect FBS accounts for a while, so met an increasing number of the farming community individually, as well as collectively, as I now got caught up in the 'talks and conference circuit', both at home and overseas.

As already indicated, after about 1970 the need for 'liaison' began to diminish: the job, it was felt, had been done. At this point, along with other FMLOs, I became 'absorbed' into my Department with a gradually increasing teaching load and a renewed commitment to research which had taken something of a back-seat during the busy 'sixties. Neither of these developments, however, seriously reduced my contact with farmers and farm managers. Many of them were helpful in allowing me to take students for 'practical' classes on their farms and I met many others as my main research interest (still concerned with the *people* in the industry) switched from farm workers to farmers and farm managers. As I write, in 1995, I note that the results of my first survey of *the work and pay of farm managers* was published in 1970 – and that, twenty five years later, I am working on the seventh!

Looking back from this perspective, it is clear that whilst I changed universities only once, my 'job description' changed numerous times and was certainly very different during the 'seventies and 'eighties from how it looked in the earlier 'liaison' years. Sometimes the changes occurred suddenly, – as when I moved to Reading in 1960; but more often, gradually as when liaison work slowly petered out ten years later. At all stages, as one door closed another opened. Increasingly, however, it was to be the other way round, as new responsibilities meant relinquishing earlier ones. But at no stage were my links with the farming community discontinued. As the pattern of work changed, new opportunities presented themselves to continue a dialogue that had started in Gloucestershire in 1953. And even as successive promotions brought increased administrative responsibilities in my Department, in the Farm Management Unit and in the University more widely, that dialogue continued until retirement – and (I am pleased to say) beyond. A more detailed account of the various circumstances in which it took place belongs to the next chapter.

●●●●●●●●●●●●●●●●●●●●●●●

Largely to bring the situation into focus for myself, I have, by way of an appendix to this Chapter, illustrated in Table 1, below, the way in which *changing responsibilities influenced my opportunities to meet the farming community*. The dominance of advisory and farm survey work before 1970, and of teaching, research and the talks/conference circuit afterwards, will be clear. No mention is made here of *administration* which occupied more and more time in the later years. Enjoyable as some of it was, however, it reduced rather than increased the opportunities for discourse with farmers.

**TABLE 1 Opportunities provided by working commitments to meet farmers and managers 1953-1993**

| Broad area of work | Activity | The 'Liaison' Years | | The 'Academic' Years | | |
| --- | --- | --- | --- | --- | --- | --- |
| | | Bristol 1953-59 | Reading 1960-70 | Reading 1971◄--1980--►1993 | | |
| PAES work | Advisory work | ● | ● | ● *(reducing)* | ○ | ○ |
| | FMS and other survey work | ● | ● | ● *(reducing)* | ○ | ○ |
| Academic work | Teaching | ○ | ○ | ● | ● | ● |
| | Research | ● *(labour oriented)* | ● *(limited)* | ● | ● | *(reducing)* ● |
| Outreach work | Extra-mural talks | ○ | ● | ● | ● | *(reducing)* ● |
| | Conferences | ○ | ● | ● | ● | ● |

Key: ● = Good opportunities within 'activity' to meet farmers/managers
     ○ = No or minimal involvement in activity

# 4 Where and When

**THE VARIABLES**
The previous two chapters have explained 'how and why' I came to be in close contact with farmers throughout my career: how I came to be an agricultural economist and, within that broad discipline, how I came to specialise in farm management. *This* chapter moves the story on to say something about 'where and when' contact was made. The circumstances were immensely varied – and I have often threatened to write a book about them!

Broadly speaking, the variation has been in three directions:, *professional, numerical* and *physical* – and each of these 'variables' affected each of the other two. *Professionally,* encounters ranged from confidential discussions about a particular farmer's financial concerns to speaking very generally in front of a conference audience of several hundred. *Numerically,* therefore, it follows that my 'meetings' with farmers have ranged from very personal encounters with individuals to very impersonal encounters with large audiences which, in addition to farmers, farm managers and sometimes their wives, would usually have included a cross section of other interested professionals – such as advisers, bankers and accountants. So, *physically* speaking, there has been an equally wide variety of meeting venues, ranging from the farm office or kitchen to conference centres and civic halls.

Within each of these three variables – professional, numerical and physical – the broad spectrum of situations alluded to above has, over the years, embraced a highly varied collection of individual circumstances – far too numerous and varied for them all to be mentioned, but which I have tried to summarise in Table 2 below:

**TABLE 2 'Meeting' Farmers: A Summary of Circumstances**

| Face to face | | | | Small or medium sized groups | | Large gatherings | |
| Alone | | With others | | | | | |
|---|---|---|---|---|---|---|---|
| Activity | Location | Activity | Location | Activity | Location | Activity | Location |
| Collecting Survey Data | Farmhouse - office | Student visits | Farm, barn | Talks/ Lectures | Farmhouse, Pub, Hotel, Local Hall | Con- ferences | Conf Centres, Univ/Coll, Hotels, Civic Rooms etc |
| Other Research | Farmhouse - office | | | Seminars | Hotels, Univ/Coll, Meeting rms | | |
| Advising | Farmhouse - office | Advising | Farmhouse - office | Farm walks | Farm, barn | Farm walks | Farm, barn |
| Socialising | Farmhouse Bar Restaurant | Socialising | Farmhouse Bar Restaurant | Committees | Boardroom Offices etc. | | |

As the reader will observe, the initial division in the table has been threefold, roughly according to the numbers involved: *either face to face* (with or without others), in *small or medium sized groups*, and in *large gatherings* – and each of these three has been further subdivided according to the main *activities* and *locations* involved. The purpose of this Table is simply to summarise a very mixed bag of situations and no hard and fast boundaries are inferred.

## FIELD WORK

The first three activities in the left hand column – collecting data, research and advising – have much in common with each other and, more often than not, have taken place 'in the field' in a face-to-face situation, without the presence of others. Without doubt it has been those situations, more than any others, in which I have genuinely 'got to know' the farmers and managers concerned – and they, me.

Often recurring annually, distinctions between professional and personal matters have, over time, become blurred, as confidences have been exchanged and good friendships made. If I have been of any help in these situations, then I have also been helped, and most of the quotations that appear in the next two chapters of this book have emerged in the intimacy of those discussions and the socialising that has often followed.

I was, of course, also often in these situations as part of a team, especially in my early 'liaison' years, accompanied by a local advisory officer and perhaps by a banker or accountant. And since the onlooker often sees the best part of the game, it was not unusual for the farmer's wife to be present. Without doubt, this made me aware of the role, both active and passive, played by farmers' and farm managers' wives in the management of many farm businesses, and it was perhaps no accident that my first research report to be published under the banner of the University's Farm Management Unit was on that particular subject[10]. Mainly, however, meeting farmers in the company of others belonged to the activities listed in the right hand side of Table 2: at evening lectures, at conferences and on farm walks – and I will return to those subjects shortly.

## FARM VISITS AND WALKS

But, first, a word about taking students on farm visits. Successful farm visits do not occur by accident. They need to be well planned, with the farmers clearly knowing what is going to happen and what their own role will be. A number of the quotations in the following chapters have come from farmers'

---

[10] The Farmer's Wife: Her role in the management of the business (with W I Buchanan and A J Errington). FMU Study No 2, The University of Reading, 1982.

replies to the questions raised by students and have therefore been well honed as the visits and questions have been repeated year after year.

My colleagues and I have been very grateful to the many local farmers who have been prepared to repeat these exercises – in some cases for *many years* – sympathetic to young people who, especially the budding agricultural economists, have had little or no prior agricultural knowledge. For the occasion to be more than 'a jolly' away from the lecture room, it is important for a class to be well briefed about who they are going to meet and what they are going to see and, especially, to know that, in one way or another, a commitment is required from them – such as keeping an ongoing log book and perhaps having to answer examination questions based on the visits. I believe that the farmers appreciated knowing this and for many years it was my practice to persuade some of the host farmers to come to the university, a week after the visit, for a considered discussion away from the inevitable distractions of the farmyard. These farmers were not chosen at random; they had something to say and knew how to say it. Meeting and listening to them was, to my mind, an important part of a student's education. For their part, farmers, without exception, have been kind enough to say that such occasions have been of value to them, causing them to think clearly about their own businesses and personal objectives in order to answer 'critical' questions from intelligent young people.

For me, quite apart from the friendships I have made, regular visits of this kind over many years have been invaluable as a painless way of keeping a finger on the pulse of the farming industry: essential in the teaching of farm management.

Incidentally, it may have been noticed that in my summary table I have included student visits in the category of 'face to face with others' because that's how it was for me. I was not facing the students, as in a lecture; rather, facing the farmer, often prompting the discussion in what I believed to be the 'right' direction, whilst encouraging the students to join in: not always easy if they are conscious of their own lack of knowledge, especially in the face of fellow students from a farming background who often need to be held back a little in a 'muddy boots' environment with which they are familiar.

At this point I must make a confession which I would never disclose to students. Whilst I have always enjoyed taking students on to farms I have to confess that (as my colleagues know well!) I have had a limited appetite for more general farm walks. I have seldom felt this to be inconsistent with my long-standing interest in the broad sweep of the countryside – often, in my opinion, better viewed from a motorway than from many farm tracks! A notable exception to this has been on the University's saucer-shaped Churn farm – sadly to be sold at around the time this book is to be published – with its unrivalled images of the Berkshire Downs. Perhaps my general attitude towards many farm walks, however, stems from my own lack of agricultural training, but so often I have found them to be poorly organised, time consuming and given over to too much technical minutiae that has often failed to excite my personal curiosity. On the whole I have found *listening* to farmers more interesting than *looking* at their farms, and farm walks (especially in inclement weather!) are often not conducive to listening. The situation was rather different in the case of advisory work when a *short* farm walk was an essential part of the piece – but even then, I must confess, primarily as an opportunity to listen to and help build up an impression of the 'client'. It was, of course, also necessary in those circumstances, quite apart from appearances sake, to display *some* interest in the farm as such but I was always happy to keep it short and, if possible, to be left alone for half an hour or so with the farm accounts, perhaps while the farmer and his technical adviser, if he was present, enjoyed a lengthier walk of the farm. On their return I was usually ready to make the points or ask the questions that I felt were relevant and which I would not have gleaned from simply walking the farm. Proof of the pudding, after all, is in the eating!

There are, of course, exceptions to every rule, and before leaving the subject of farm walks, I must in fairness to myself, say how much I have valued the more 'private' version, designed for a small group, with a clear objective – whether it is structured or unstructured. A good example of the more structured form has been the annual two-day Study Tours for members of Reading's Farm Management Unit. Superbly organised by Malcolm Stansfield, with a tightly packed farm visiting programme designed to see and hear about what is new, these occasions have been invaluable both as in-service training and as an opportunity for hard working colleagues to relax amongst themselves and with their hosts. During the course of the last seven years these visits have taken colleagues away from the routine of academic corridors to look at farming and other rural developments, successively in Brecon, Shropshire, Yorkshire, Kent, Suffolk, Somerset, and Hampshire.

Less structured have been the days that I have spent annually, usually with colleagues Malcolm Stansfield and Peter Cockburn, visiting close friend, Andrew John, on the farm he now manages on the Cotswold outlier of Bredon Hill (see cover photograph). With nothing firmly on the agenda, we have just walked (or driven!) around the farm and talked management: an invaluable day, in good company, to recharge batteries and stimulate thought.

**CONFERENCES**
Over the years I have probably met more farmers at residential and day conferences than anywhere else – but am conscious of the love-hate relationship I have had for these occasions. Whether designed primarily for farmers or for my fellow agricultural economists, I have never quite been able to reconcile some magnetic attraction that, on the one hand, has drawn

me towards conferences (often as an organiser, as well as a delegate) with, on the other hand, a need to 'escape' from them. Some of the attraction has undoubtedly been the opportunity to meet friends and colleagues and to demonstrate a genuine desire to 'belong' to a particular professional community or grouping; reflected also in the fact that in several cases I have chosen to write histories of the organisations concerned[11]. On the other hand (stemming perhaps from early National Service days, I intensely dislike communal living (other than with my wife!) and, in the interests of self-preservation, have always needed to be selective, especially at residential conferences, about the number of individual conference papers I have attended and those I have skipped. Farmers en masse are perhaps no more appealing than any other large homogeneous group, and the ability to 'slip away' to nearby counter-attractions has always been important to me; essential, in fact, to preserve sanity! Locations in the middle of attractive towns or cities seem to me, therefore, far preferable to the modern-day hotel-come-conference centre (no matter how good its facilities) stuck on an out-of-town roundabout! Over the years in this respect – first with the Agricultural Economics Society and more recently with the CMA nowhere has appealed to me more than Harrogate, rivalled only by the location of the Oxford Farming Conference meeting, as it does, amongst the city's 'dreaming spires'.

In case these views strike the reader as in any way irresponsible I should, in self defence, and before concluding this passage, say that I have always quite seriously viewed attendance at conferences as more than a mere paper-listening experience: rather, as relief from routine, a chance to recharge batteries, to socialise with friends and to enjoy fresh environs – whether home or abroad. And, if professionally, I have also come away with one or two good new ideas I have been well pleased. As a valuable antidote to routine and isolation, conferences can be a helpful experience for anyone. As it happens, few sectors of the community are more prone to routine and isolation than farming and I have often encouraged farmers to sample the conference remedy; remembering always that conferences themselves need to be 'managed' and not to be too frequent or too long!

## ONE NIGHT STANDS
Major conferences, however, where attendance is measured in *hundreds* rather than *tens,* are seldom the place where individuals can get to know each other or have more than a passing exchange. It is the smaller gatherings, typified by the many evening meetings attended by farmers, up and down the country or, by the more structured seminars often held in

---

[11] The author has written histories of the Agricultural Economics Society, the International Association of Agricultural Economists, the Centre for Management in Agriculture and the Oxford Farming Conference.

agricultural colleges and universities, that encourage more serious exchanges between those attending, as well as between the audience and speaker. I have often marvelled at the farming community's propensity to attend such meetings – attributing it in some measure to the need to counteract the isolation that afflicts farming – both physically and intellectually.

My own 'annual reports' tell me that, over the years, I have been privileged to have been the *speaker* at something like four hundred such meetings with audiences usually ranging from between twenty and forty. I have, therefore, 'met' around 12,000 farmers and managers (plus any others who were present) in these particular circumstances: circumstances conducive to a level of discussion not possible at farming's larger jamborees.

Those readers who have also 'trod the boards' on this farming circuit will know the scene well, knowing that no two venues or occasions are quite the same. One learns not to be 'thrown' by the size of the audience or the meeting room – both often either much smaller or larger than anticipated – nor by the often seemingly unrehearsed nature of chairmen's introductions and, later, the votes of thanks! I have actually been introduced *and* thanked by the wrong name although not actually on the same night! Meals before the event, with one or two committee members, can be both painfully drawn out (while one resists giving a preview of one's talk) or painfully hurried so as not to keep the audience waiting. More often than not there will be no facilities for using visual aids – and, more than once, I have managed to illustrate a gross margin on the small hinged blackboard on the side of a darts board! And when question-time comes, one learns to be wary of the questioner, often near the back, who prefaces his question 'with all due respect to the speaker, Mr Chairman, ………'!

In case it is thought otherwise, I must state that the previous paragraph was in no way meant to be disparaging; on the contrary the occasions in question are recalled by the writer with a good deal of affection – and despite long journeys, often in the worst of the year's weather – I have never not enjoyed any one of these evenings. At an early stage, I was helped by the realisation that these were not occasions to try to teach in any formal sense: rather to share one's way of thinking ( in my case as an economist) about problems that those in the audience might have. For their part, the audience usually seemed glad to have a speaker and would, therefore, be *wanting* to listen to you – as part and parcel of their social evening out. I have often felt that, on these occasions, interaction *between* members of the audience is at least as important, if not more so, than between the audience and speaker. This is even more true when small groups of farmers and managers are together in a seminar situation – when the speaker 'tutor' is often acting only as a catalyst, whilst participants share common problems and anxieties and, hopefully, solutions.

To return to the 'one-night-stand', however, I must confess that the further I was away from home (with the evening, therefore, already 'gone') the less anxious I seemed to be to get on the road home. A chat in the bar – sometimes with those who were too shy to ask questions in the meeting – was then a prelude to an unhurried drive home with the radio and heater full on! One hundred miles each way was my limit without a night stop – which commitments the next day usually precluded.

Inevitably, there were those particular occasions which stand out in the memory – usually when something unusual or amusing happened. I shall, for instance, never forget the foggy night, some thirty years ago in Reading, when I was one of three speakers (together with a banker and an adviser) and just one farmer turned up! The three of us asked him about his farm and *he* became the speaker with an audience of *three*! I have remained eternally grateful to him for preventing a situation in which *nobody* has turned up to listen to me! Another small turn-out occurred when I was booked to speak in Marlborough to the Farm Secretaries Association drawn from three counties. Anticipating a large and all-female turnout, I was wrong in *one* respect – there was an audience of four! It was perhaps the only occasion when, after the talk, the speaker has bought a round of drinks for the entire audience!

Two other experiences that I recall with amusement, when there *was* an audience, occurred in Somerset and in my original home county of Kent. Invited to speak to the Somerset Branch of the FMA (as it then was) by the then lecturer in farm management at Cannington College, I was greeted only by his apologies and the message that he had to play in a darts match: a man, I remember thinking at the time, who had his objectives clear! Then there was the Treasurer of Kent's FMA who, having ascertained my fee, divided it by the number of people in the audience, collected the appropriate levy from each of them (in a cap) and then (instead of writing the expected cheque) tipped the contents into my coat pocket. I can still see the uncomprehending look on his face when, with as straight a face as I could keep, I asked him if he would like an encore!

What *must* take pride of place in my memories, however, is a talk that I didn't actually give, following an invitation from the Warwickshire branch of the FMA to speak on 'How to Increase Profits'. There was nothing subtle about the suggested title which, incidentally, underlined why it was my policy on all such occasions to charge a modest fee. When I explained to them that my fee (at the time) was £10, they replied in writing saying that they had no money. I would normally have left the matter there, but could not resist writing back telling them that they clearly needed this particular talk very badly, and that when between them they could muster £10 I would be pleased to give it to them. I never heard again except, on the grapevine, to hear that their branch had been wound up – hardly surprisingly, I felt!

I have many more tales of this kind – often concerned with the need to adjust to the unexpected – but will stop there, before I cause offence, if I have not already done so. But no offence, I assure the reader, has been intended. I have often been privately amused but, as already noted, have *never* not enjoyed these occasions, and have always learned something *from* each one, if not about the subject, then about the questioner or about myself. I learned, in particular, that audiences and farmers are much the same wherever they are. I have sometimes been warned in advance that this or that particular audience (often in the remoter parts of the UK) will 'gobble you up'. The reality, however, has been that I have never found this to be the case – even on occasions when I suspect that I deserved it. My reference to 'partition', for instance, fell very flat when I spoke in County Armagh, close to the border between Ulster and the Republic of Ireland, to an audience which was seated in a cowshed on either side of a central dividing wall which prevented one half of the audience from even seeing the other! The silence with which my comment was greeted surprised me, having previously spent four years as a student in the Province and therefore understanding something of its humour. But they were sensitive times and I learned the lessons not, as a visitor, to tread on politically sensitive toes; just as I had learned earlier on that the speaker has the last word and should never use his privilege to humiliate a questioner, whatever the provocation.

**OVERSEAS**
Finally, here, I should say that although most of my public speaking was in the UK, professional travel took me into every continent of the world. With some reservations, however, about how far one could be of any help in other countries without actually living in them, I accepted few 'working' assignments other than to lecture. Travelling, therefore, most often as a delegate and/or a speaker to international conferences or training sessions, I found only limited scope for seeing much of the farming or meeting many farmers in the countries concerned. Despite invitations to do so, I have been reluctant, therefore, to talk publicly on my return home about the farming I have seen (or, more correctly, not seen!) around the world. Instead, I decided to build up a single lecture – which I added to as my journeys multiplied – entitled 'Travel and My Attitudes to It'. This enabled me to range over the whole gambit of my experiences – social, political and agricultural – including the sometimes stark impact of arriving home.

Apart from the warm friendships that developed on these occasions with fellow travellers, there were usually a *few* opportunities to visit farms and to meet farmers in host countries. Inevitably the farmers were hand-picked in much the same way as the locations for student visits are hand-picked – the main purpose of such visits being to see and learn from the best. Perhaps what I learned more than anything was that a 'good' farmer is a 'good' farmer wherever in the world he operates: and that, despite any language difficulties, he is usually easy to recognise the moment he begins to speak: and sometimes before!

Looking back on these various contacts with the farming community at home and abroad, I have been struck by the fact that however serious the business, humour has never been far away. Over the years I have heard many funny things said, and feel that I cannot close this particular chapter without recounting two of them that continue to make me smile. One occurred close to home, in Reading, and the other, far away in South Africa.

I first met Berkshire farmer, Peter Strang, back in the 1950s when for several years he and I played rugby against each other for Berkshire Wanderers (now Reading) and Clifton respectively. After I came to Reading, Peter was very helpful for many years in welcoming student classes on to his farm, at that stage on the very outskirts of Reading. In due course he had to move further out to make way for Courages Brewery and when I asked him (in front of students) how he felt about that he replied, in his droll way, that 'it was exchanging one good form of land-use for another'!

Further from home, I was travelling, in 1983, with Vic Hughes, then Principal of 'the Royal', whom I had previously not known well. The two of us had been invited by John (Butch) Harrison – who I had previously worked with during my Bristol days when he was at Newton Abbot – to join forces on a lecture tour of South Africa, sponsored by the South African Farmers Weekly. Independently, Vic and I had each asked Malcolm Stansfield how he thought we would get on travelling and working with the other! Reassuring us both, Malcolm is, therefore, indirectly responsible for the friendship I have enjoyed with Vic ever since. My wife, who hails from Johannesburg, came with us as we criss-crossed the country by air and land for two weeks. One journey was from Middelburg to Port Elizabeth in a small car without air conditioning, directly across the Karoo desert in intense heat. Vic was 'first on' the next morning and endeared himself to the farming audience with his opening statement that he had often been told to go to hell, and now he knew where it was!

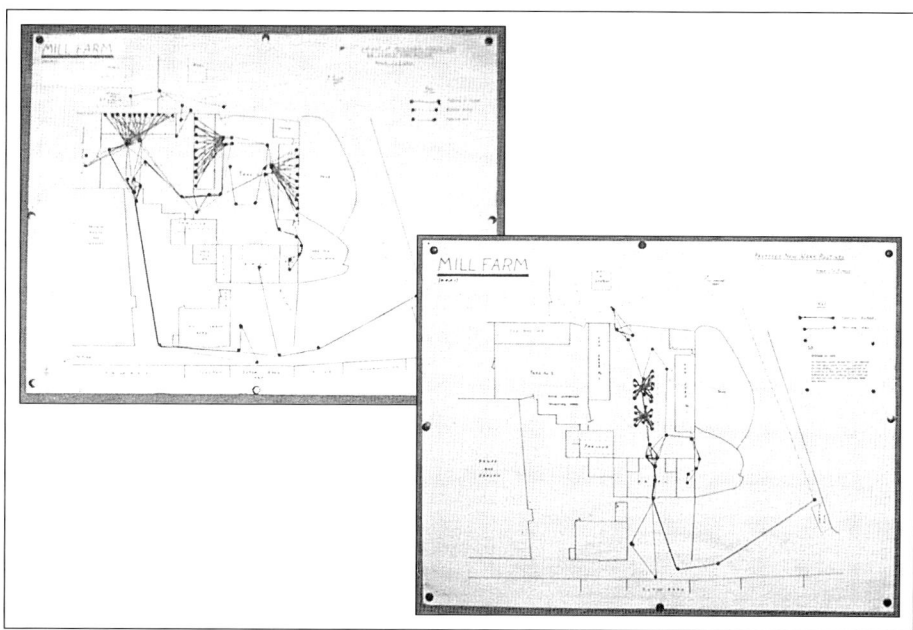

1  String Diagrams at Bristol: 'Before and After' cattle feeding routines, mid 1950s.

2  Extract from first Farm Management Handbook prepared by the author at the Department of Agricultural Economics, University of Bristol, 1955.

DAIRY FARMS UNDER 100 ACRES

Production and Cost Structure

| | 1952-3 | | 1953-4 | |
|---|---|---|---|---|
| Production (Per Acre) | Average | Above Average | Average | Above Average |
| Cattle | 3.0 | 4.9 | 3.6 | 4.6 |
| Milk | 32.7 | 42.8 | 33.4 | 42.4 |
| Sheep and Wool | 0.15 | 0.2 | 0.1 | 0.3 |
| Pigs | 1.8 | 2.4 | 2.6 | 3.8 |
| Poultry and Eggs | 1.35 | 1.6 | 2.2 | 2.6 |
| Horses | 0.0 | 0.0 | 0.0 | 0.0 |
| Crops | 0.9 | 1.3 | 2.05 | 1.95 |
| Sundries | 1.5 | 1.7 | 1.7 | 1.95 |
| Total Production | 41.4 | 54.9 | 45.65 | 57.6 |
| Costs (per acre) | | | | |
| Wages (1) | 5.7 | 6.2 | 6.3 | 5.9 |
| Purchased Foods | 11.7 | 16.4 | 12.7 | 15.6 |
| Crop Expenses: | 1.5 | 1.4 | 1.55 | 1.05 |
| (Seeds) (2) | (0.7) | (0.6) | (0.5) | (0.3) |
| (Manures) (2) | (0.7) | (0.8) | (0.8) | (0.75) |
| Rent | 3.0 | 3.1 | 3.2 | 3.5 |
| Power and Machinery | 4.2 | 5.3 | 4.45 | 5.4 |
| Miscellaneous (3) | 4.7 | 5.2 | 4.75 | 5.75 |
| Total Costs | 30.8 | 37.6 | 32.95 | 37.3 |
| Gross Profit or Loss | 10.6 | 17.3 | 12.7 | 20.3 |
| Value of Farmer's and Wife's Labour | 5.8 | 5.6 | 5.9 | 7.0 |
| Investment Income | 4.8 | 11.7 | 6.8 | 13.3 |

(1) Paid Labour plus unpaid labour other than farmer's and wife's.

(2) Seeds and manures although shown separately are included in Crop Expenses.

(3) Includes contract and hire.

3 Author's first attendance at the Oxford Farming Conference, Town Hall, 1960.

4 Author's first overseas farm tour, Queensland, following the 13th Conference of the International Association of Agricultural Economists in Sydney, 1967.

5 Another Oxford Farming Conference, 1975 – where the author has met farmers and farm managers for 35 years, giving rise to the name 'See You at Oxford!' for his history of the Conference published in 1995.

6   Ex-chairmen of the FMA/CMA (l to r): Graham Dalton, Vic Hughes, John Nix, Peter Street, Frank Paton, Mike Fort, Peter Innes, Malcolm Stansfield. Seated: Nigel Agar and Derek Pearce, 1982.

7.  With farmer Gordon Lugg and farm manager Luke Wishart: the Working Party to manage CMA's independence from BIM, 1987.

8   Serious business at the 1987 CMA Conference; the Chairman listening to the Secretary, Philip James.

9  The Farm Management Unit's first Study Tour, to Wales, 1990. In truck (l to r): Neil Ravenscroft, Peter Cockburn, David Ansell, Rupert Loader, Andrew Errington, Dick Esslemont, Peter Dorward and Tahir Rehman. Standing, the author and (right) the host farmer. (Stansfield took photograph).

10 Typical farming audience in discussion after farm walk: the CMA national farm walk, at Leckford Estates, 1990.

*11 The only known farming photograph taken by the author! A sheep station in the North Island, New Zealand, during 8th International Farm Management Congress, 1991*

*12 Author presenting the 9th Edith Mary Gayton Memorial Lecture at The University of Reading in 1992, his valedictory year; close friend and colleague Malcolm Stansfield in the chair.*

13 The 'Edith Mary Gayton' audience: a mixture of farmers, colleagues, agronomists, students, relatives and friends, 1992.

14 Off duty in Poland: with Malcolm Stansfield, David Ansell and Tahir Rehman on a working assignment to the University of Olsztyn, Poland. Photographed with interloper, Richard Rampton from the Berkshire College of Agriculture, 1992.

15 The best type of farm walk! With FMU colleagues at the University's Churn Estates, 1993.

16 Extract from last of 37 Farm Management Handbooks prepared or edited by the author, Farm Business Data, 1993, Dept of Agric. Econ. and Management, The University of Reading. An interesting contrast with photograph number 2.

| Group 1: Specialist milk, producers, 50 ha or less (less than 20% arable) | | | |
|---|---|---|---|
| | 1990 | 1991 | Prem.* |
| Number of farms | 17 | 17 | 4 |
| Average size of farms (ha) | 33.4 | 33.3 | 39.4 |
| | average £/ha | average £/ha | average £/ha |
| **Total farm output** | 1,872.2 | 1,918.0 | 2,581.0 |
| **Variable costs** | | | |
| Feedstuffs | 544.5 | 490.7 | 701.6 |
| Seeds | 6.6 | 9.9 | 14.3 |
| Fertilisers | 87.5 | 78.8 | 128.6 |
| Sprays & other crop costs | 12.9 | 15.8 | 14.9 |
| Casual labour | 20.3 | 13.1 | 20.1 |
| Contract charges | 77.2 | 75.7 | 98.4 |
| Vet and medicines | 39.0 | 47.7 | 59.7 |
| Other livestock costs | 146.2 | 163.8 | 182.9 |
| **Total variable costs** | 934.2 | 895.5 | 1,220.5 |
| **Total farm GM** | 893.0 | 1,022.5 | 1,360.5 |
| **Fixed costs** | | | |
| Rent and rates | 131.7 | 132.2 | 144.8 |
| Labour | | | |
|   Regular paid | 61.3 | 59.4 | 94.1 |
|   Unpaid | 349.6 | 366.5 | 319.0 |
| Power & machinery | | | |
|   Fuel & electricity | 64.2 | 66.8 | 61.5 |
|   Repairs & insurance | 75.6 | 84.1 | 87.4 |
|   Depreciation | 111.1 | 105.0 | 127.6 |
| Occupier's repairs | 40.1 | 23.7 | 27.8 |
| Sundries | 98.9 | 109.7 | 119.1 |
| **Total fixed costs** | 932.5 | 947.4 | 981.3 |
| **Management & investment income** | -39.5 | 75.1 | 379.2 |
| Average tenant's capital | 1,970.0 | 1,903.0 | 2,467.0 |
| Return on above capital | 0% | 4% | 15% |
| New machinery investment | 102.0 | 36.0 | 40.0 |

\* Premium 1991 top 25% of farms

17 Farm Management Unit's retirement party for the author at the Visitors Centre, Sonning Farm, 1993. Faces visible to the camera include, John Miller, Gordon Machin, Author, Gordon Lugg, Andrew John, Dick Dancey, Richard Clarke, Heather Giles, John Nix, Steve Wiggins, Peter Street, Ray Carter and Bill Richardson.

18 Oilmen or farmers? Reading University's Farms Manager, Peter Cockburn, talks to his opposite number on an FMU Study Day in the Midlands, 1994.

*19 Chairman of the Organising Committee checks the details with CMA Chairman, Devon farmer, John Carter, at opening reception of the 10th IFMA Congress at Reading University, 1995.*

*20 In retirement on his allotment, where, says Malcolm Stansfield, 'the author has at last learnt something about soil chemistry!', 1995.*

# 5 How They Manage

If the previous chapters have been autobiographical in tone, with pronounced use of the personal pronoun, I can only plead some inevitability, as I set out to explain how I came to be so involved with the farming community. In keeping with the sub-title of this book, however, I can promise that the following chapters will be different, focusing more on the business of management, on some individual farmers and farm managers I have known and on what some of them have said to me, in their wisdom, about farm management.

Clearly, farmers and farm managers do not have identical roles. Farmers are self-employed, with their own capital at risk, and ultimately have responsibility for all that happens in their businesses; farm managers, by contrast, are salaried, with delegated responsibility, and have their jobs, not their capital, at risk. Despite these differences, they do, however, have much in common – at least on a day-to-day basis – and I will not, therefore, in discussing their attitudes to management, continue to make a clear distinction between them or refer to them both when wanting to refer generically to those who *manage farms*. I will refer simply to *farmers* or *farm managers,* as suits the text and will, unless stated to the contrary, be meaning both groups; they do, after all, both farm and both manage!

It is widely agreed that all managers – whatever they are managing – have much in common. *Management* is *management,* I have often argued, whether it is of farms or any other activity, and the reader should not, therefore, be surprised if few of the quotations from these 'farmers' make much, if any, reference to agriculture as such – and that most of what is quoted would be equally applicable to the management of any business or organisation. They are, after all, the words of men who manage businesses that happen to be farms: Managers as Farmers. Perhaps I should add that I have also included here a few of my favourite quotations from general business management literature which, conversely, are just as applicable to the management of farms as they are to the general business and industrial setting in which they were originally written or spoken.

It follows from all this that much of what is contained in the next three chapters, in particular, will have a strongly anecdotal flavour, and that it called, therefore, for some orderly presentation which I have tried to provide by the chapter headings: *How they manage, What they manage,* and *No man an island.*

Some readers (especially if close to Reading!) may spot that in following this sequence I will be doing no more than broadly following the sequence of the diagram in Figure I that Malcolm Stansfield and I first used for the layout of our book: *The Farmer as Manager*. It was a diagram that we jointly forged, as co-authors, setting out what we saw as the main *responsibilities* of any manager (setting objectives, planning, taking decisions and controlling things, i.e. the *how* of management); the main *segments* of any business that have to be managed (production, buying and selling, finance and staffing, i.e. the *what* of management); plus the multifarious nature of the wider environment within which managers have to do their job in practice.

**FIGURE 1 The Framework of Management**

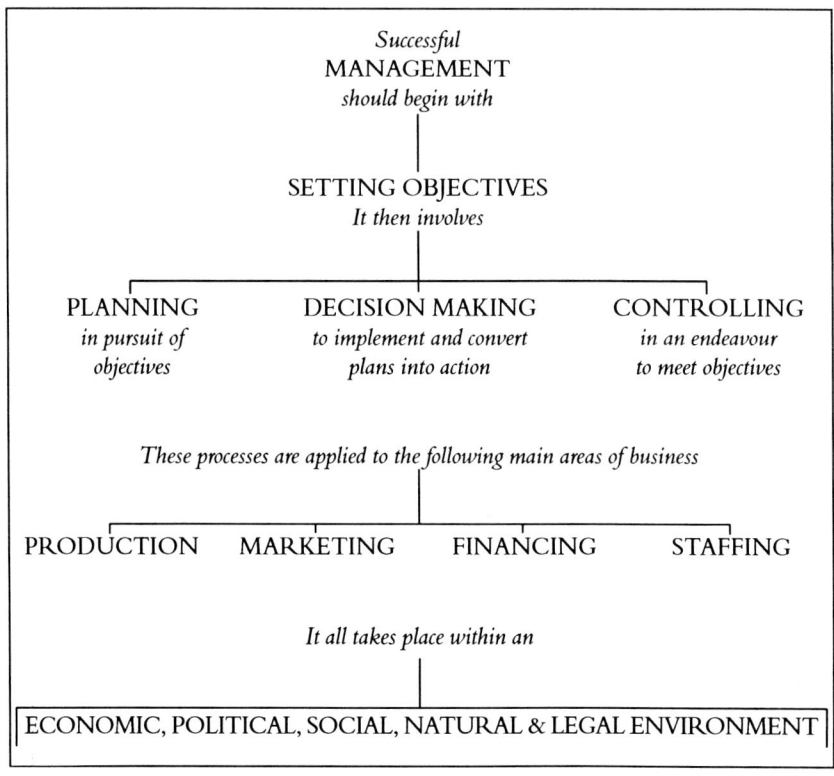

Since this is not a text book, and since the 'ins' and 'outs' of the diagram were discussed at length when it first appeared in 1980, the author has no intention of going over it again here. For the same reason, as the text proceeds in this chapter and the next, each aspect of management will be referred to only briefly, as a backcloth for the comments of farmers and farm managers.

Of the diagram itself, I should add, however, that it is still, fifteen years after its origins, in use by both of us and, despite many suggestions to the contrary, we have neither wanted to make it more complex by adding words to it, nor to try to illustrate, with more linking lines, all of the many underlying complexities and inter-relationships that it suggests and which we know to exist in real life. In other words, we have, over the years, *deliberately* kept the diagram simple, believing it to be comprehensive enough to provide a framework, or background, against which any particular aspect of management can be set in context and its complexities brought out in discussion.

At this point I must counter the rumour that Reading students have only to reproduce the diagram in the examination room to pass their farm management exam! But I will unashamedly admit that I have personally (and, Malcolm, no doubt, too) used the diagram in the way described above, no matter what I have been leading on to, time and time again at farmers' meetings and in lecture rooms. So much so that one university colleague, finding the diagram on every blackboard when he followed me into a classroom asked (with tongue in cheek?) if I only had *one* lecture! My answer was firmly 'no', but that I did have one overall *framework* against which I wanted to set any particular aspect of management that I was going to talk about: the *framework* against which the rest of this chapter and the next two are set.

## MANAGEMENT

It may have been noticed that the first word in the Giles/Stansfield diagram, prefacing the word 'management', is the word 'successful'. It is axiomatic that anybody managing anything will set out to do it successfully. In the words of American businessman and author, Robert Townsend:

> *'If you can't do it excellently, don't do it at all. Because if it's not excellent it won't be profitable or fun and if you're not in business for fun or profit what the hell are you doing here?'*[12]

Of course, not everybody in farming (or anywhere else) will be doing it excellently nor even, judged by the range in published performance figures, successfully. Within the limits of their own capabilities and resources, however, everyone will at least be *trying* to be successful knowing that a continued lack of success can only have one end. The author cannot call to mind anybody – farmer or otherwise – who admits to not *trying* to be successful, and certainly not anybody who admits to deliberately trying not to be! In practice, of course, plenty of us manage not to be successful (if that is not a contradiction in terms!) with everything that we attempt; but, hopefully, with training, experience and guidance, improvement may come over time.

Years ago, however, I recall a particular farmer, in the less hospitable parts of north Buckinghamshire, who, year after year, managed to make a loss – and

---

[12] 'Up the Organisation', R Townsend. Michael Joseph Ltd, 1970.

each year for a different reason. In my relative inexperience at the time, I knew that I had failed to address his problems tactfully and constructively enough, when he looked me straight in the eyes and said:

> *'You think I'm a bloody awful farmer, don't you'*

He was a particularly nice man and I had learned an early and valuable lesson in the need to try, at least, to say unpalatable things in a palatable and constructive way.

There are many definitions of what successful management is or should be; perhaps as many as there are authors who have written about the subject, or managers who practise it. In my experience, however, whilst many good farmers have clear ideas about what is required in specific areas of management – whether technical or financial, few of them are equally clear about the *totality* of the job; too busy, no doubt, getting on with it than to have time to theorise about it! As sheep breeder Oscar Colburn (and member of the already mentioned Cygnets discussion group) concluded in his delightful book – Farmers' Ordinary:

> *'....as ordinary farmers await the next set of (market) signals, they milk the cows, feed the sheep and prepare for seed time and harvest.'* [13]

Aware, however, that in practice, the farm manager – depending upon whether he is self employed or salaried, is responsible for most if not all aspects of the business, Giles and Stansfield arrived at the following definition to supplement their diagram:

> *'Management is a comprehensive activity, involving the combination and co-ordination of human, physical and financial resources, in a way which produces a commodity or a service which is both wanted and can be offered at a price which will be paid, while making the working environment for those involved agreeable and acceptable.'*

If fifty-two words seems over-long for a definition, what else could be expected in reaching a compromise that would satisfy an academic economist and a practical farm manager turned lecturer?! Although deliberately shorn of all references to farming – for reasons already given – this statement was deliberately worded to emphasise four aspects of farm management that we believed to be of paramount importance: first, its *totality* or *comprehensiveness;* secondly, that management is concerned with *combining* different factors of production; thirdly, that there must be a focus on *end products* and fourthly, there must be awareness of the *human* dimension.

---

[13] 'Farmers Ordinary'. O Colburn, Alexander Heriot, 1989.

Whilst this description of management seemed appropriate for a text book it was, of course, too much of a mouthful to trot out in conversation with farmers or even when addressing a local meeting of a couple of dozen farmers in the back room of their 'local'. On those occasions, since a definition is usually a good starting point, I would personally rely more on an altogether briefer definition, often drawn from general management literature. One of my favourites has been:

> *'Management is deciding what to do and then doing it'.*

Despite its brevity, this statement says it all – and applies in all situations. What it does not do, of course, is indicate what is involved in the process of either *deciding* or *doing*. Another favourite, therefore, which took the definition a little further, was:

> *'Management is the art of making good decisions based on inadequate information from dubious sources.'*

I confess to not remembering where this definition first came from, but over the years it has allowed me to 'moralise' about certain of its words such as 'art' (rather than science), 'good' (rather than best), 'inadequate' (rather than complete) and 'dubious' (rather than gospel). I imagine that we all find ourselves in the position of this definition, whatever we manage. And certainly, it never failed to raise smiles and discussions with a farming audience whenever I invited them to focus on their responsibilities in directing, planning and controlling their businesses.

## SETTING OBJECTIVES

The theme of the Centre of Management in Agriculture's annual conference in 1995 was *Managing for the Future,* and its Chairman – the genial Devonshire arable and pig farmer, John Carter, – opened proceedings by warning his audience that:

> *'If you don't know where you are going, you might end up somewhere else!'*

No doubt words like this – or similar – have often been uttered before – but they were well chosen on this occasion, being at the heart of what this conference was about: the need for strategic thinking and clear objectives for the future.

Whether borrowing management techniques from other industries – such as Management by Objectives, Total Quality Management, or any one of several other similar techniques – or whether relying on more informal round-the-table farm-house discussions – there is as much need for this fundamental aspect of management in farming as in any other industry: perhaps more so bearing in mind the relatively lengthy production cycles that characterise much of agriculture. Acutely aware of the conflict between *getting things right in the long term* and *keeping things right in the short term,* it was Berkshire farm manager Tim Culley (whom I have known for many years) who once shrewdly reminded me that:

> *'Farming is a long term activity in which the short term demands so much attention.'*

Setting objectives – especially for the long term – is not easy. It can be time consuming, difficult to be precise, and the situation will constantly be changing, calling for periodic review. There will be conflict between individuals, competing enterprises within the business and, as Tim Culley reminded us, between the long and the short term. The process, however, is essential in order to give any business a carefully considered purpose; to give individuals within the organisation a common and understood approach to the work, and to minimise the risk of going off at too many tangents which may be undermining survival.

In an informal way – harnessing the help of others inside the business, together with sympathetic professionals who are outside – many farmers will be familiar with this sort of thought process, not least when they consider annual cropping and stocking programmes and forward budgets. Many, however, will not take the process far enough or will skirt round it altogether, with a preference for rolling up sleeves and *getting on with the job.* They will not be alone in this attitude – but they could be (and many *have* been) left behind in the survival race. It may be hard to convince everybody, but a substantial investment of thought and time is worthwhile if only to arrive at what, at the end of the day, might be a quite brief, but agreed statement about the *main purpose* of the farm business. From a statement of that kind, much of value can follow about *how* and *when* it can be achieved and, if necessary, how modified in the light of changing events.

In case it is thought that this kind of approach is a product only of recent years, the author has never forgotten one of his earliest face-to-face meetings with a farmer, soon after starting out at Bristol University in the early 1950s. The farmer in question was Wilfred Cave, one of Wiltshire's best known pioneer farmers of the pre and post war era. With his natural willingness to encourage the young, he had kindly agreed to help me with one of several labour studies with which my colleague and friend, Bill Cowie, and I had begun to make our professional way together at Bristol. This particular study was to be called 'The Farm Worker: His Training, Pay and Status', which we approached through the use of 'structured interviews' with a small hand-picked group of farmers, known for enlightened attitudes towards employment[14]. It was an education to talk and *listen* to them – and more of their collective views anon. In the context of *setting objectives*, however, I am still waiting to hear a clearer and more enlightened statement than Wilfred Cave's when he said:

> *'My objective is to run a farm that is successful enough to pay top-class staff top-class wages.'*

Perhaps not dissimilar (but more starkly stated) was the more recent statement by Hampshire's Gordon Machin – kind enough to let me take Reading undergraduates to him for over twenty years. Like Wilfred Cave, he broke away from a family farm and, in the days of low land values and rents, set out at an early age on his own with strictly limited capital and equally limited agricultural training. With a natural affinity with big machines, Gordon (now in the process of relinquishing hands-on control) approached his all-arable farm with the disarming philosophy that:

> *'I farm for profit and dislike all unnecessary work!'*

Student eyes would be out like organ stops as his invariable first answer to their questions about why certain things were done in a certain way, was *'for profit'*! Here was the 'economic man' of their text books – but Gordon's more human philosophy would always follow. Recent terms such as 'mission statement' and 'preferred future' may have recently replaced 'management by objectives' but they all amount to the same thing – and the need for them seems greater as time passes rather than less.

## PLANNING

Our diagramatic management framework tells us that the first step towards achieving *objectives* is careful *planning* – to the point that the dividing line between the two processes is sometimes difficult to draw. In particular what the two processes have in common is that they occur (or *should* occur) *before* events happen. Planning, especially, is like that: it is about making arrangements before something happens so that it happens the way that is wanted, and not in some other chance or haphazard way. In practice, many things, of course, do not happen precisely as planned; but that is never a good reason for not planning – original plans can be modified in the light of events and activities kept as close as possible to original or modified intentions.

In the farming scene, planning is often thought of as being synonymous with *the* farm plan and with production. The reality, however, is that the

---

**14** This report, in a 'neutral' cover, was not published until 1964, several years after I had left Bristol for Reading, and shortly before Bill left for Newcastle. It is referred to in more detail in Chapter 6.

planning process is as necessary with each of the other main segments of the business – marketing, financing, and staffing – as it is for production. In each segment, however, planning is the antidote to so-called 'management by crisis' – characterised as that is by moving from one crisis to another, often without the learning of lessons.

Planning may not be a particularly exciting aspect of management and, in my experience, is not something that (apart from the farm plan) farmers talk much about. One incident, therefore, that stands out very clearly in my memory was when a Canadian farmer (whose name I never knew) talked to me in the bar after I had addressed the Alberta Farmers' Conference at the Banff Conference Centre in 1982. This annual conference is rather like a Canadian four-day version of the Oxford Farming Conference – except that it is attended, in the harsh winter months, by all of the family. Many of the papers had a rural sociological flavour and I could not help noticing that as the days wore on there were more farmers' wives left in the auditorium than farmers! My subject was The Farmer as Manager (the book having just been published and selling well in Commonwealth countries). I stressed the importance of planning. The farmer who then approached me in the bar wanted to tell me how pleased he was that I attached so much importance to this particular aspect of management. He went on to explain that with his land snow-covered for long periods in the winter, he and his two farming sons spent long hours planning the next season's activities – and always felt slightly guilty about it because they were not obviously 'working' ! I assured them that they were – very importantly – and that they should not feel guilty in any way. It is a feeling that I have often come across in the farming community – especially amongst the young – that no real work is being done unless sleeves are rolled up and that one is out of the office. Over the years, I have done all that I can to dispel any such attitudes. But what is true, of course is that planning is totally unproductive work if decisions are not subsequently taken that put plans into effect.

## DECISION-MAKING

There are those pundits in the management world who virtually equate decision making with management itself. Important as it is, I cannot, personally, see management in such limited terms, preferring to regard each item in the *framework diagram* as important parts of a 'jigsaw puzzle' that would be incomplete without any one of them. It is true, of course, that many managers do spend a lot of time (and worry) making decisions; and while they may delegate some of the routine day-to-day decisions that have to be taken within individual farm enterprises, at the end of the day they have the final responsibility for these as well as for the more strategic decisions about directions and priorities. Remember that one of my favourite definitions of management referred to *'the art of making good decisions with inadequate information from dubious sources'*.

However adequate, or not, the information, and however dubious or not the source, it is nevertheless an inescapable feature of decision-making that decisions usually have to be taken in the present, based on information from the past, about events that will occur in the *future*. It is also the case that wherever a choice exists, it is only the outcome of the chosen course of action that is known. To that extent it can never really be claimed that the *best decision* has been taken – only the one that *appeared to be best before the event*. American management guru, Peter Drucker, advises against haste when important decisions have to be made and includes 'learning to make good decisions' in important situations amongst the five habits of mind that managers should cultivate in the process of learning to become *effective*[15]. In essence this particular habit requires a sequence of: recognising important issues, identifying and evaluating alternative courses of action (or inaction), followed by implementation and acceptance of responsibility for a chosen preference.

This methodical but realistic approach reminds me, incidentally, of two professorial Heads of Department at Reading with whom I especially enjoyed working: Ronald Tuck – not unknown for taking his time – who, sometimes after several hours of discussing some important issue would say:

*'Well, we've done all we can to get that right so what more can we do?'*

– and his immediate successor, my close friend John McInerney, who enjoyed reminding himself, and others,

*'Not to let the best be the enemy of the good.'*

Against the background of this brief account of the nature of decision-making, I am conscious of the *many* interesting statements that I have heard from farmers about decision-making, in contrast to the *few* I have ever heard about planning. Perhaps this confirms the nagging insistence with which this part of management does, in fact, dominate much of their work. Decisions, decisions, decisions......... Several statements stand out for me, like Reading University farms manager (and good friend) Peter Cockburn's acidic reminder (to us all!) that:

*'We are not where we are by accident'*

but, by inference, as the result of past decisions or indecisions.

---

[15] The Effective Executive. P F Drucker, Heinemann 1967 and Pan Books 1970. (The other good habits of mind are: knowing where time goes; focusing on results; building on strengths, and staying with priorities.)

I have learned much from listening to Peter, as I have from two other close friends in the farming community – neither of whom came directly from a farming background, Andrew John and Richard Clarke. Disenchanted with the 'city' life to which he was first directed, Andrew emigrated to Canada where he worked as a 'mobile cowboy' for two years before returning to attend Shuttleworth College. After working his way up the farm management ladder, he managed the large Home Farm on a prestigious estate close to Reading before moving to a similar but larger responsibility in the heart of the Severn Vale. Richard Clarke, by contrast, was a Reading graduate who, because of the illness of the manager, found himself (not altogether fortuitously) promoted to manage a large multi-enterprise farm on the Berkshire Downs – before, later on, setting out on his own.

Both of these able managers – in some respects the archetypal managers as farmers whom this book is about – found themselves with major managerial responsibilities at a relatively early age, directing staff who were old enough to be their fathers, if not their grandfathers! Of course, they made wrong decisions but, all importantly they learned from them; Richard freely admitting that:

*'I've learned more from my mistakes than from what I got right.'*

and Andrew acknowledging that:

*'My experience is the accumulation of my mistakes.'*

Finally, under the heading of decision-making comes warning from Poul Christensen – a good friend of the University of Reading (and of the author) and much sought after for his wisdom (and good humour) on agriculture's current political stage. Farming with his sons in Oxfordshire and the West Country, he faced important strategic decisions during the anxious years of the 1980s and early 1990s – from which farming may only have temporarily recovered – and cautioned himself (and others, in the course of his public speaking role) that:

*'Anxiety is the worst possible position from which to make decisions.'*

A salutary warning indeed.

## CONTROL

It has seldom been my experience to see enterprises being conducted on farms that are not suitable for them. This is not surprising. The farming community is, generally speaking, well informed and able – entirely capable of assessing what makes sense for their farms and themselves. What is not so uniformly the case, however, is the ability to manage well the enterprises that have been chosen. This situation is not peculiar to farming but, rather, reflects the normal range in human ability which manifests itself in any trade, industry or profession. In farming, more than anything else, it explains the well-known range in performance levels that were referred to earlier in the chapter.

I believe that at the heart of this phenomenon is the question of control: that aspect of management that aims at ensuring that what has previously been planned, decided upon and implemented does, in fact, happen – as closely as possible to what was intended and at a stipulated level of efficiency.

There are, of course, all sorts of factors at work which are outside the control of the farm manager which will affect performance levels (in both directions!) – the weather and Government policies to name the most obvious. But their existence is not a reason for not trying to control whatever aspect of the business remains controllable. In many situations there are more of them that is popularly imagined. Control will be both physical and financial: supervision of what is physically going on, on the one hand, and careful budgetary control matching performance against targets – on the other.

More often than not the explanation for disappointing profits (assuming that the farm is large enough or intensive enough to be capable of producing them) lies not, therefore, in *what* but in *how* things are being done: either in terms of scale or within the cost/benefit ratio. Early on in my Bristol days, when being 'tutored' by Stuart Wragg, I recall a farmer once saying to him during a follow-up visit *'I can't understand what went wrong: we did nearly everything that was suggested'*. As we drove away I also remember Stuart saying 'the trouble was he did *nearly* everything, not *everything*! '. Fixed costs are not called 'fixed' for nothing; they tend 'to hang around' and must be offset by the appropriate number of productive units performing at the required level. *Control* – physical and financial – is about trying to ensure that that happens. As such, it should be close to the heart of every farmer: it is, after all, about getting things done, at the right time and well – and not allowing the 'good' to mask the 'poor'.

The direct relevance of this aspect of management to the attainment of pre-determined objectives and plans made me, personally, more enthusiastic about it than virtually any other part of business management. But I *never did* believe (and, despite the advent of computers and information technology in all its glory, I still *don't* believe) that it need be over-complicated or conform to some uniform set of procedures. We all live in a world in which there is a clamour for more and bigger *data bases* – as opposed to a small and manageable amount of *information* immediately relevant to the individual and the question in hand. Information technology and modern methods of communication will have their places, but managers must be careful not to spend more time looking into a screen than they do at the livestock and crops and the men and women upon whom so much depends for success. So before I get 'carried away' on this score, let me record the pleasure and amusement I derived from the answer that one pig farmer gave to my 'planted' question in front of a class of students. The late Andrew Melville and his son Richard have been pioneers amongst pig breeders and producers in Berkshire. I took students to their farm over many years, not least (and with *no* disrespect whatsoever) to see that a farm didn't necessarily have to be covered in whitewash to produce good results. Both father and son were busy people and kept the frills, in every respect, to the minimum. Their major enterprise, however, was pig rearing and fattening, in which small profit margins leave little room for manoeuvre. Anxious, therefore, to let the students understand that careful budgetary control was important and that this probably called for extensive recording systems I asked Richard:

*'What records do you keep to control your pig enterprise?'*

to which he replied (to my delight, and quite unprompted!)

*'As few as possible.'*

– and he was right, of course!

# 6 What They Manage

*Setting objectives* is usually associated with the periodic need to identify long term strategies and targets and may, therefore, come on to the management agenda only occasionally. By contrast, the other three aspects of the manager's job that were discussed in the previous chapter – planning, decision-making and control – will be altogether more immediate and continual, and relevant to whatever segment of the business has to be managed – day-by-day, week-by-week and month-by-month.

In most (but not all) cases there will be four such segments or main areas of activity: production, marketing, finance and staffing. For the purposes of understanding, it is convenient and conventional in most management writings to consider each of these segments separately. In doing the same here, it is important, however, not to lose sight of the fact that, in practice, each is closely and inextricably related to each other in a variety of ways. A range of inputs, for instance, will be purchased in the *market* place in order to *produce goods* and services that will, hopefully, be sold in other *market* places and, in the process, *cash* will flow in and out of the business as *staff* are employed to add value in the *production* process. So as we go on now to consider each segment of *what has to be managed*, we should not over simplify in our minds what we know, in reality, whether in agriculture or elsewhere, to be an intricate and inter-dependent set of circumstances.

## PRODUCTION
As already inferred above, production is essentially about transformation: the transformation of a given 'bundle' of resources into something else. In farming terms this means combining the four classical 'factors of production' – land, labour, capital and management – into commodities (traditionally basic foodstuffs, but increasingly a more diversified range of goods and services) for sale at a price that someone else will be prepared to pay. It is, incidentally, sometimes overlooked in an industry that is characterised by uncertainties that, because of the essential nature of food, the amount, in total, that populations are prepared to pay for it is unlikely to either fall or rise dramatically. This 'inelastic' demand for food provides, for farming as a whole (if not for individuals), a safeguard against the severest buffeting from an adverse economic climate.

But I digress – if only a little. In order to determine their production programme, farmers have to answer the three questions posed in the economist's so-called 'theory of the firm': what to produce, how to produce it and how much to produce? In farming terms this means: what farming (or other) enterprises, by what husbandry methods, and on what scale and in what combination will each be produced. The answers to these questions will then give rise to a production plan which should indicate what inputs (in addition to the fixed ones) need to be brought in. The production plans themselves can be derived in a variety of ways, ranging from fairly subjective decisions, such as a farmer simply saying to himself that 'I want to milk 100 cows and put the rest of the farm into corn', to the use, in complex situations, of sophisticated computerised techniques. The plan, especially its cropping element, will certainly be reviewed annually, although, in overall composition, is unlikely to be subjected to *major* changes too often. The possibility, on the other hand, of advantageous *marginal* changes, hopefully tested by partial budgets, will be constantly passing through the manager's mind and may be introduced at any time.

At this point I am reminded of the evening when I was speaking to a farming audience about farm planning and budgeting, stressing my belief that it need not be a complicated task – only to be taken to task by one farmer who said critically *'you make it sound so easy'*, to which, after a pause, I found myself replying *'Would you like me to make it sound difficult – academics have no trouble in doing that!'*.

More particularly, however, mention of partial budgets reminds me of a sheep farmer in New Zealand's South Island whom a group of UK delegates visited on the way home from Sydney, after attending the thirteenth conference of the International Association of Agricultural Economists in 1967. He was describing a major change to his farming system and, knowing that any change brings its own difficulties, one of our group asked the farmer why he was bothering to do it. I remember his reply, word for word, to this day. Without a smile and looking rather like an All Black prop forward, he said, quite slowly but without hesitation:

> *'Because I feel the harsh lash of the economic whip on my back!'*

Each word registered like a nail being driven into wood.

Of all aspects of management, I have always believed that the actual physical production of their output – crops and livestock – is closest to most farmers' hearts. That is why they are there, preferring the practical farming to anything else whether they are specialists, concentrating on a chosen enterprise, or spreading their knowledge and energy over several. The choice between specialisation and mixed farming can be a difficult one to make and what exists may often be a second-best compromise. One of my favourite examination questions has been:

> *'Many farm systems are the result of a compromise between a desire to specialise and a need to diversify. Discuss.'*

Incidentally, many of the examination questions that I have set over the years have originated from comments made by farmers on farm classes. To my lasting amusement, however, one originated from a comment by a coach driver who had driven us to a farm. Quite often these drivers (some of whom have previously worked on farms) would walk around the farm with us and on one such occasion the driver, having listened carefully to the farmer talking about his difficulties, said quietly to me 'There are no black and white answers here – its all trial and error isn't it? '. I latched on to his comment and the exam question became:

> *Farming often depends upon trial and error rather than text-book answers. Discuss.*

The strongest case that I ever heard made by a farmer for specialisation came from Sam Brooks, who lived on a large Cotswold farm north of Cheltenham. He also had a smaller dairy farm in north Bucks which (interestingly) he farmed at an arms length, visiting the resident stockman only once a fortnight. Sam had come out of the Royal Navy after the war and started farming with no agricultural knowledge, but with clear views about the management of money and men – some of which he had learned in the Navy. Taking over the mixed arable and livestock farm in Gloucestershire he soon converted it to an all arable system, saying:

> *'I am concentrating on what I think I can do best and in the process expect to get better.'*

It was amusing to listen to him describe how much farming literature did not, therefore, concern him and could go straight in the waste paper basket. He was, incidentally, the only farmer I ever met who used to 'close' his farm. On one occasion, before setting out to visit his brother in Australia, he wrote to all and sundry, including MAFF, telling them that his farm would be 'closed' for a stipulated time during which they could expect no replies from him! 'Shops close', he used to say, 'so why not farms?'

Many other farmers, of course, prefer mixed systems of farming and do so for a variety of reasons, often technical and financial, as well as to spread labour requirements throughout the year. Others are diversifying well beyond traditional farming enterprises and I have often hankered after arranging what would be a fascinating day tour within a ten mile radius around Reading that would encompass such 'non farming' activities as selling antiques, picture framing, storing caravans and boats, art galleries, winemaking, farm shops, iron work …… and numerous others. A recent two-year study by Exeter University found that over 40 percent of all holdings in England and Wales had at least one non-farming enterprise, with as many as one third of all holdings in the UK having diversified in some way.[16]

---

[16] Patterns, Performance and Prospects on Farm Diversification. John McInerney and Martin Turner, The Agricultural Economics Unit, University of Exeter, 1991.

Whatever the arguments for or against these diversified activities there can, therefore, be no denying their popularity, especially where a graduate son or daughter wishes to cut his or her commercial teeth on the farm, but outside the farming. In one instance it will work, perhaps utilising slack resources, while in another it may not, only interfering with the continued improvement of what already exists. A cautionary note to this effect has often been sounded by farmer, John Miller, when talking to Reading students. Farming on the outskirts of Reading with a mixed arable/livestock system – and with a healthy range of personal interests that help to get him off the farm, he believes that:

> 'The best form of diversification is to do what you are already doing, better.'

In other words, an *improved* enterprise can be a *new* enterprise, and managerial effort and know-how will not have been dissipated. What is important in all this is that, in deciding on his production programme, each farmer must decide what is right for him given his own farm, his own interests and talents and the other resources at his command. Perhaps the last word here should, therefore, go to the previously quoted Poul Christensen who insists, simply:

> 'That you should not take on what you can't manage.'

## MARKETING

There are many in the management world who would not wish to differentiate much, if at all, between so-called *production* and *marketing*. They see both as part and parcel in a long chain of 'transformations', starting with the purchase of inputs and ending with the end-product in the consumer's hands. In contrast, others, including most farmers, I think, would see a fairly clear dividing line between physically producing something *on* the farm and selling *off* it. To an extent this is to deal in semantics and this author is prepared to argue the matter both ways.

Historically, the majority of farmers have, and many still do, concentrate most on the physical production, and a long history of guaranteed markets has made them relatively disinterested in the marketing process; something, they have felt, that belongs more to the realms of the professional salesman.

In reality, all farmers are, and always have been, involved in marketing whether they know it or not and whether they like it or not – the prices they receive in any situation (as well as the prices they pay) being important ingredients in their profit formula. It would be foolish, therefore, for them to expend valuable effort and know-how in 'producing' commodities at the physical end of the job, only to neglect the other – the selling. It is, incidentally, important for them to remember that they are also involved 'in the market' as buyers, usually more often and across a wider spectrum, than they are as sellers. With profit margins usually a relatively small residual amount, after total costs have been subtracted from total sales, this situation is inevitably the case, and has caused at least one well known farmer – Oliver Walston – to stress the importance of careful buying. It also caused Malcolm Stansfield and me to include a chapter in the *Farmer as Manager* on *buying and selling* rather than *marketing,* in the belief that farmers generally would identify more closely with those two functions than with the more generic term, marketing.

In essence, we argued in that book that farmers have to address three main marketing questions: what products are they going to produce and by what methods; what selling outlets are they going to use; and how far do they personally wish to become involved in them? To take milk as one example, a farmer may choose to produce low-fat milk, peaking in the autumn and winter months, to a major wholesale dairy with no personal involvement other than as the physical producer. By contrast, his neighbour may produce high-fat milk, with the emphasis on summer production, to produce dairy products on his own farm for sale direct to retail outlets including the public. Both will have made decisions which will affect what they *do* on the farm, the income they receive from their chosen *outlet* and the extent of their personal involvement. The paths they have chosen will differ from each other, but both, in their different ways, will have made marketing decisions – even if some of them look more like production decisions.

With very clear indications that agricultural policy in Europe and elsewhere is moving towards financial support for the industry that will be part and parcel of social and environmental mechanisms, directed towards individuals or areas in need rather than to the market place, there is equally clear evidence that many farmers, especially as they diversify, are now more alert to the importance of marketing than they were a mere decade or more ago when they were urged from every platform to 'improve your marketing'.

It was not uncommon to find farmers in those days who were perplexed by that clarion call, asking themselves and others 'what can I do that I am not already doing?' Today the answer to their question has become clearer and, as we have seen, will be different for different individuals, ranging probably from 'not much' to 'plenty' – depending upon the enterprises involved and the willingness of individuals to get involved, or not, towards the consumer end of the food chain.

Against this background, it must be said that the author has heard few statements from farmers over the years about marketing that qualify for quotation here. Instead, he has come to rely more on general marketing literature – of which there is plenty. It is a subject that lends itself to slogans, usually somewhat tedious references to phrases like 'the *right* product, the *right* time and *right* price ...... etc, etc.' My personal favourite, from an unknown source, but much more pithy, has been:

*'If nobody sells, nothing happens!'*

– and by inference, of course 'if nobody buys'.

Perhaps not surprisingly, therefore, my one marketing quotation, originating from my direct contact with 'agriculture' comes from horticulture not farming: a sector in which the lack of guaranteed markets combined with the variety and perishability of its output has required a far more market-oriented entrepreneur than has been the case in much of conventional farming. The quotation comes from Peter Gray, a fruit and vegetable specialist in business with his father (a pre-war graduate of Reading University). Joining his father near Wokingham, following marketing experience outside the industry, Peter manages a dozen or more crops which are sold both on and off the farm. For many years he has welcomed student visits from Reading's budding agricultural economists who have been made acutely aware during the visit of the intricacies of juggling with double cropping, cash flows and conflicting labour requirements in this type of business. A regular question from the students is 'How do you decide which crops to grow?' and the reply embraces the essence of all good marketing:

*'I only grow what I know I can sell'*

– not what he hopes, or thinks he can sell, or what he is told he can, but what he *knows* he can.

With his PYO operation alongside his external outlets, Peter Gray would no doubt agree with my other favourite marketing slogan:

*'Good marketing is when the customer comes back but the product doesn't!'*

## FINANCE

Financial management is a huge and complex subject: whole books have been written about it even in an agricultural context. Here, we have a quarter of a chapter to consider it! The need, however, to say or write something that is meaningful, within a short space about such a large subject, is not an uncommon experience for many speakers and writers, and I have personally often found the answer in the use of some diagramatic device. In the case of *financial management* the idea for such a device came to me years ago in the middle of the night, sometimes a good time and place for uncluttered thinking!

What came to me on that occasion was the thought that the subject can be divided into two, twice: once in terms of *time* – the past and the future (at any point of time all financial transactions have either happened or are going to happen, so the 'present', in this context, doesn't exist), and once in terms of subject matter: trading and capital considerations. Transposing these thoughts into Figure 2, below, it will be seen that all aspects of the subject (records, accounts, budgets, balance sheets and investment, etc) can be placed appropriately in one of the four segments of the diagram. The subject is thus encapsulated in a logical and manageable way.

**FIGURE 2 What Financial Management Involves**

|  | The Past | The Future |
|---|---|---|
| **Trading** | Records<br>Accounts | Budgets<br>Cash Flows |
| **Capital** | Balance Sheets | Investment<br>Appraisal |

For reasons given earlier on in this chapter it is not the author's intention to go into any of these topics in detail in this book beyond a brief word to reflect a little of my approach to them. Some of them will be touched on again, anyhow, in Chapter 9 on 'cornerstones and beliefs'.

Past trading is all about records and accounts and my approval, in the last chapter, of Richard Melville's attitude to pig records, says much about my own approach to *record keeping*; an approach, incidentally, over which I have often suspected my stable-mate, Stansfield, thinks I am a bit cavalier! But keeping records can be a time consuming and costly business, so I believe they should be restricted to those that are *needed* and *used* either by the farmer himself (or those acting for him) or to meet some statutory or other specific requirement. Economist and journalist, George Schwartz, was correct when he wrote, years ago, that:

*'the cost of keeping costs down is going up all the time'!*

He was right then and would have been even more right now. A good test of any record is to ask how much better the planning, decision-making or control processes have been as a result of having it.

The appropriate financial records are of course necessary for the construction of a trading account and good management accounts will require more detail than those required by the Inland Revenue. If they show the annual output from each enterprise and the level of the major inputs then, following the kind of sequence shown in Figure 3, the appropriate calculations and comparisons can help to indicate where improvements and adjustments are desirable. But all of this is only an aid to good decision making, not a substitute for it.

**FIGURE 3 A Systematic Management Analysis**

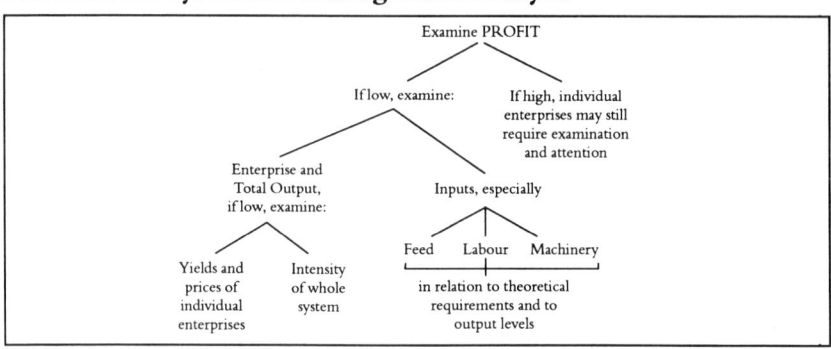

If *past trading* is recorded in accounts, then *future trading* is forecast in various kinds of *budget* relating to all or part of the business or any particular input, including cash. My views about budgeting are straightforward: it is not easy (although costs *are* generally speaking easier to forecast then receipts) but it is easy to neglect. The fact that there are unknowns and uncertainties – or that things never work out as forecast – are not good excuses for not *trying* to get it right: for trying 'to muster all the accuracy one can', as my colleague Alan Harrison used to say. The alternative to budgeting, of course, is not to budget and simply to hope for the best – perhaps to be disappointed, too late. Remember from our discussion of setting objectives, if we are not prepared to form a view of the future we have no right to be surprised by its outcome.

Turning now to the *capital* part of our diagram, *past capital* is recorded in the *balance sheet* which, if kept up-to-date, provides a valuable picture of the make-up of assets and liabilities in a business and the all-important difference between the two – its Net Worth: the owners stake in his or her own business. Like record-keeping, however, the balance-sheet analysis can easily be allowed to get out of hand. There are, to my view, only a limited number of balance sheet ratios that need to be understood; essentially those concerned with the dangers of high gearing (heavy borrowing with high interest charges that have a first call on profit margins), vulnerability in the event of called-in loans, and over-investment in non-income earning assets.

Finally, in this section, a word about *investment appraisal*, where future capital is considered. With so much of farming's capital in the form of land or other fixed assets, this is probably the most important part of all financial management. The introduction of fresh capital provides the golden opportunity to change direction or to expand and improve what already exists. These are opportunities that cannot be wasted and I have (with tongue partly in cheek) suggested to farming audiences and student classes that I could teach them most of what they need to know about investment appraisal by inviting them to do one simple thing and then to ask one question:

> *Take a good look at the person next to you and imagine he or she has asked you if you would lend them £1000 (or whatever figure seems appropriate to the circumstances) – and then ask yourself what thoughts pass through your head?*

Those thoughts will be precisely the questions that a bank manager will ask a prospective borrower: What for? What do I know about you? Who else is involved? What interest should you pay? When will the the money be returned, etc etc – investment appraisal, in its simplest form!

If required to speak more formally on the subject, without venturing into the intricacies of formal investment appraisal, I have suggested a check-list of ten questions to be asked before embarking on any significant investment:
1  Is the investment necessary to achieve your objectives?
   (The answer may be 'no', but if 'yes')
2  Have you budgeted, however crudely?
3  Is the investment income generating?
4  Is there a certainty (or just a hope) of return?
5  Are you 'playing to your trumps'?
6  If a new activity, have you researched it well enough?
7  How long will you have to wait for your return?
8  If necessary, can the investment be liquidated for use elsewhere?
9  Are you keeping the amount and cost of borrowing to a sensible minimum?
10 If it is a so-called 'labour-saving' investment, how is the saving to be made?

I have 'dined out' in the farming community on the strength of this list many times – including once that I remember so well for reasons other than my talk. It was in a hotel on the outskirts of Andover aerodrome. Financed by a major bank, it was an evening meeting at which there were six short talks of which mine was third, followed immediately by a liberal supper and drinks interval. Relieved to have done my bit, I concentrated more on the liquid than the solid refreshment and then took my seat near the front of the very crowded room from which easy exit was difficult. In the event, the second three speakers dragged on and, as my personal discomfort level rose, I vowed never to make the same mistake again!!

Returning to more serious matters, there are many reasons offered for the high stress levels that are generally associated with farming. High on the list are financial worries, often simply the nagging necessity to go on generating profits, year after year, in order to survive. It is not surprising, therefore, that plenty has been said to me by farmers on this score, and which I could quote. They range from the calming comment from the previously quoted Andrew John that

> 'Money is simply a tool of management'

to the rather more anxious view of my long-standing New Zealand friend, Jim (Sir James) Stewart, that the three things that matter most in managing a farm business are:

> 'Cash, cash and cash!'

Andrew John's comment carries with it the inference that money represents the command over all of the other resources – land, labour, machines, stock – which, in practical terms, are the ones that have to be managed; while Jim Stewart's stems from his own farming activities that he carried on alongside, successively, his Chair in Farm Management at Lincoln College, his Vice Chancellorship of that University and his knighthood. Years previously, Jim had arrived at Reading (to take a doctorate) at the same time that I arrived in 1960. We shared a common interest in farm management, rugby football and young families. He has kept in touch on numerous visits to this country and I have been able to visit him in 1967 (at the time that I met the 'harsh lash of the economic whip'!) and again in 1991 when the International Farm Management Association (IFMA) held a congress in both the North and South islands of New Zealand.

On a similar theme, but on a different level and in a different country, I cannot easily forget the farm manager (who, for reasons that will be obvious, cannot be named) who invited me to his farm to talk things over because he was worried about the future. In anticipation of the visit I was allowed to examine the trading accounts for the previous three years during which the profits were consistently very high by any standards. Asking him why, therefore, he was worried, he replied:

> 'Because I need to keep them that way!'

The moral of this story is don't wait to ring the Samaritans before it is too late: an attitude that was also brought home to me by Lindsay Edwards, a charming and welcoming Hampshire pig farmer. He was no doubt expressing the views of many who, over the years, have taken part in the university-based Farm Business Survey, when, in answer to my question as to why he bothered to do so, he replied:

> 'Because once a year, whether I feel like it or not, it ensures that I have to get to grips with and concentrate on financial matters which might otherwise be neglected.'

Another Hampshire farmer, Eric Chase, provided an object lesson in a very important area of financial management – keeping within budget. A post-war Reading graduate, we had numerous interests in common including playing cricket and, now that Eric is in retirement, writing. Farming with his brother, their mixed dairy and arable farm was an excellent example of how good (as opposed to astronomic) yield levels combined with well controlled fixed costs can *consistently* produce better than average results. I remember in particular, when, in the mid-seventies, inflation was passing 20% and Eric said simply:

> *'I beat inflation by not spending!'*

Let me hasten to add that Eric Chase was, and is, a generous man with whom I am glad to remain in touch; but he had a clear-cut and, therefore, relaxed business attitude.

His approach was not unlike that of Poul Christensen who took delight on the occasion of student visits to his farm in pointing out the dangers of making *spending* economically respectable by labelling it as *investment*. I think he felt that economists were responsible for this deception – but 'not this one' I had to assure him! It was implicit in my 'check list' that investment should be kept to a necessary minimum by careful scrutiny, if not by formal appraisal, and I was always at pains to point out that the 'necessary minimum' depended very much on the individual and the scale and style of what he might be contemplating. Having made this point (I thought very clearly) at one evening talk, I was saddened when one questioner (whom I can visualise as I write) said *'I am thinking of starting a pig unit – how much capital do I need?'* I think I resisted replying 'the price of one pig and its feed' – but that's what was going through my mind!

Finally, in this financial section, I should say that I cannot recall any worthwhile remarks from farmers about *balance sheets*; perhaps because the notorious strength of farming's balance sheet tends not to give rise to the nagging burden of the profit and loss account. This section would not be complete, however, without some reference to the infamous *gross margin*: and here I must quote the shrewd and down-to-earth Mike Limb, Director of the Royal Agricultural College's farms around Cirencester, who some years ago said to me:

> *'It is no longer good enough to think that a gross margin of £1000 per hectare must be good business without careful thought about the fixed costs.'*

How right he was – and more about that in a later chapter. But here, reference to gross margins reminds me of my favourite examination question which was:

*No examination paper in farm management would be complete without a question on gross margins. Set one and answer it.*

I remember one external examiner (who should have known better!) taking me to task over this, believing it to be a 'cop out' on my part. It was nothing of the sort; rather, a question on which it was easy for the superficial student to hang him or herself – some of whom did!

## STAFFING

After the rather lengthy section on finance, this one can be briefer: not because it is in any sense less important – on the contrary – but because what is really important can be said fairly briefly.

The number of employees working on many of Britain's farms is small and is constantly reducing. The working relationship between employer and employee is, therefore, often a close one and, over the years, labour relations in the industry have, generally speaking been good. As the much respected Berkshire dairy farmer, Jack MacDonald, once put it:

> *'There is no great personal difficulty once two people know they can work together; if they can't the relationship won't last anyhow'.*

Almost certainly, however, such a blissful state of affairs does not exist in all situations and there can be little doubt that the close employer-employee relationship in farming, which often extends outside working hours and even into the domestic sphere, contains its own peculiar problems. It is important, therefore, that farmers and farm managers should not rely on good labour relations through default, but should give careful consideration and continual thought to their staffing needs and practices. Much, in terms of the success of the business, is at stake and there could be no more important aspect of management to which they should devote their attention.

This view was expressed at its most positive nearly fifty years ago by Cotswold farm manager and, later, Norfolk farmer Derek Pearce – first known to this author (as noted earlier) as a member of the Cygnets Discussion Group. Unusual as a British farmer, in having attended the Harvard University Business School, he was the author, in 1958, of one of the earliest books on farm management[17] in which he wrote that:

> *'All on the farm must share an enthusiasm for productivity, progress and profits. This attitude can only emanate from the top, whence it is diffused down through the business, finding its expression in sound and imaginative organisation and in wise and inspiring leadership.'*

---

[17] Farm Business Management: Its Principles and Applications. D G Pearce, Oliver & Boyd, 1958.

As explained earlier in this book, I have had an interest in various facets of this particular subject since the beginning of my career as an agricultural economist. And looking back over forty years of discussions about it with farmers, farm managers and farm workers, I do not think I have heard anything that has been more straight forwardly expressed than what was said in the early nineteen sixties to me and my then colleague, Bill Cowie, in the 'structured conversations' that we had leading to our publication on the 'training, pay and status' of the farm worker[18]. In a section dealing with human relations on the farm we had decided (rather than conduct yet another survey) to request what are known in the social sciences as 'structured conversations' with a number of farmers who were well known in the industry for their enlightened attitudes to employees. Going downwards in scale of operation, we selected five such farmers – Rex Paterson (in Hampshire), Wilfred Cave (Wiltshire), Hew Watt (Essex), Ted Owens (Somerset) and Jack MacDonald (Berkshire). Armed with a list of nine topics[19] we simply invited them all to talk.

The detailed reactions of each was recorded as a separate case study, followed by a summary of their combined views under each of the nine headings. In the event, perhaps the most interesting and important feature of the information collected was the similarity of the statements made despite some widely differing farming and staffing circumstances. With their acreages ranging from 8000 to 124 and the number of employees from 80 to 1 it was, nevertheless, possible to extract from the views and attitudes expressed what we referred to at the time as *'a single blueprint for successful employment'* based on the following three fundamentals.

1. By *recognising, first and foremost, the importance of employing the right type of man for the job in question – and leaving no stone unturned to achieve this successfully.*

2. By *recognising the need to retain this man (or woman) by a clear understanding of the material and personal needs of the individual with special emphasis on wages – 'not an item in the trading account to be kept to a minimum' – and (where necessary) housing.*

3. By *recognising the need to help develop the individual's talents and confidence and to create in him a sense of being an important member of a team.*

At the end of each interview, the five farmers were invited to put the nine topics in order of importance. Three of them placed 'the importance of recruiting the right kind of person for the job in question' in first place, but one, who was reluctant to suggest an order, said:

---

[18] The Farm Worker: His Training, Pay and Status. A K Giles and W J G Cowie, The University of Reading and University of Bristol, 1964.

[19] Type of worker preferred; terms of employment offered; delegation of responsibility; wages policy; housing policy; welfare; working conditions; training; personal development.

> 'They are all important and contribute to the most important factor, namely, making the employee feel that he is doing a responsible and worthwhile job and is a member of a team. He should always understand what he is doing and why he is doing it ... most men respond to this and are responsible and conscientious.'

In today's language it would be called job enrichment. As a tailpiece, let me add that one of our five farmers, Hew Watt, was presenting a paper to the Oxford Farming Conference in 1962, in which he included successful human relations as one of the three objectives of his farming policy. His vivid definition of the subject concludes this section:

> 'Human relations means talking to people and listening to them and whenever possible explaining why. It means trying to see the other person's point of view and showing due regard for it. It means the giving of promises and keeping them and less talk about 'them' and more about 'us'. The farm, to be successful, must be one big family. An employer has tremendous responsibility in this and if the day ever comes when a baby could arrive in one of his cottages without him knowing it was expected, then he is out of touch with his staff and his farming business will have lost something that no economist with his electronic computer can put back.'

If various circumstances in the industry have changed during the thirty five years since that paragraph was written, the general sentiments it expresses should not have.

One conclusion to be drawn from this chapter and the previous one is that there are many components in *what has to be managed* and to *how it should be managed*. In large organisations responsibilities for different parts of the business and different managerial functions can be delegated to specialist middle and senior managers: hence the existence of production managers, sales managers, accountants and personnel managers within such organisations. In small businesses this luxury is not possible – and most farms are, relatively speaking, small businesses. There is limited room in the industry for middle managers, which means that *the* manager, whether self employed or salaried, has the task of being directly responsible for everything that goes on. He is the production, sales, finance and personnel manager all rolled into one; a jack of all trades and, inevitably, therefore, a master of none. This is not to belittle him: on the contrary he has the most difficult managerial job of all – direct responsibility for it all. We will end here, therefore, with the salutory notice that Mike Collis the cheerful and capable manager of Reading University's Centre for Dairy Research – has above his desk:

> '*I do not have an expert, I only have myself!*'

# 7 No Man an Island

In addition to being the butt of other people's humour, economists are well accustomed to being accused – usually wrongly – of single mindedly judging every issue in terms of financial considerations alone – if not of naked profits; and, in the minds of some, 'management' is not far behind. It is always pleasing, however, to be able to redress balances (especially in the face of unfairness) so I was personally pleased when, in 1980, a teaching opportunity came my way which allowed me to function, as an economist, on a broad canvas. It now provides the ingredients for this chapter.

In the opening chapter of this book I explained how, when John Pearce retired from the University in 1979, I became responsible, as Director of the newly formed Farm Management Unit, for all of the University's farm management interests – with Malcolm Stansfield as my Deputy.

To digress for a moment, I should add here that, within that umbrella arrangement, Malcolm soon became Head of the Department of Agriculture's Farm Management Section with *me* as *his* Deputy. Each of us, therefore, was both the other's boss and his subordinate – a valuable lesson in working relationships, which could be a salutary experience for others! But perhaps it was an arrangement that could only exist in a university or similar environment.

Returning to John Pearce's departure, I found myself responsible for teaching a course, in the Spring of 1980, the subject matter of which had, by tradition, been entirely the choice of the Head of farm management. John, who was an avid European traveller, had built up a descriptive course of European agriculture covering most of its countries. From the students' point of view (final-year undergraduates and MSc students specialising in management) it was a valuable adjunct to what, in other courses, they were learning about European agricultural policy. I did not, however, have anything like the detailed knowledge of European agriculture that John had, and decided to exercise my prerogative of choice in another direction.

I had long been conscious of the fact that in the normal course of teaching farm management there is an almost unavoidable emphasis on business techniques, leaving various other topics and activities with too little attention. In particular, I felt there was a need for more emphasis on:

- the presentation of management as a *holistic* subject, as opposed to its bits and pieces (too much emphasis, as I used to say, on the individual bricks as opposed to the wall);

- the range and impact of all those influences – economic and otherwise – that are *external* to the business, but which provide the business with its opportunities and its constraints;

- the need to meet and *listen to experts and practitioners* drawn from that 'external environment', in its widest possible sense, in a setting (such as the classroom) that allows listening and encourages dialogue.

In order to meet these needs I, there and then, devised a course the underlying philosophy of which is reflected in Figure 4 below – with the farmer (or farm manager) surrounded by a series of concentric circles, suggesting diminishing direct impact from the various external influences as one moves outwards from the centre.

**FIGURE 4 Diagramatic View of the Manager's Environment**

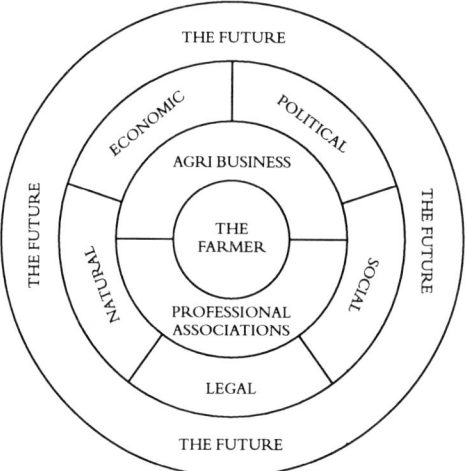

Closest to the farmer in this diagram is the world of agribusiness with which he trades, together with advisers and organisations that are directly relevant to his own professional interests. Beyond that comes a spectrum of wider, but no less important, influences – economic, political, social, legal and natural – which, in different ways, impinge upon all businesses and managers. And further out still is the unknown but constantly evolving future.

Having designed the course, I was faced with two options. I could either pretend to be an expert in all of the chosen topics, and give all of the lectures myself, or recognise that this was by no means the case, and invite the best speakers I could find for each session. Choosing the latter option proved to be the most important contribution that I ever made to the course although

I undertook to be present myself at each session, acting as the resident tutor, holding the course together and, of no little importance, looking after each guest speaker. I believe, incidentally, that a commitment of this kind from a resident tutor is important in any course relying on a range of visiting lecturers.

In that form, the course ran for fourteen years until I retired, but, in modified form, still exists as I write. Early on, one or two speakers dropped by the wayside, but before long there was a settled team of ten, including myself. Only one of them (Andrew John) was a practising 'farmer' but all of them had, throughout their careers, been close to farmers and farming and in several cases had some kind of overseeing responsibility for farms, if not for hands-on management. As a Board member of the University's Churn Estates, and holder at the time of one nominal share, I could even stretch a point and put myself in this category! Each speaker was expert in his field and, together, they made a formidable team: something not lost on the students, nor on me, for whom, each year (as when I led farm classes) was like a refresher course on the farming issues of the day. I like to feel, also, that each speaker was also my personal friend, making their annual contributions pleasant social, as well as academic, occasions. I suppose that I traded heavily on these friendships both in keeping a settled team together for about ten years and in persuading each of them, in due course, to convert their lecture notes into a chapter for a book to be called by the same name as the course – *The Manager's Environment*. In the event, seldom, if ever, have I had less trouble in extracting or editing the written word from others than I did in this case, and the book was published jointly by the CMA and the University's FMU in 1990[20].

Whilst I had a preferred order in which the sessions were presented to the students, the actual order often had to bow to the availability of these busy speakers – and somehow, with a bit of juggling of dates, we almost always managed to fit them all into the ten sessions that were available. Incidentally, when I made the arrangements with each of them over the telephone, I never indicated in which order I had approached them, not wanting the last of them to know that there was only one date left, and that I regarded him as likely to have the fewest prior engagements! In the book, however, I chose an order which reflected the pattern of Figure 4, starting in the middle and working outwards. This same order is followed in the following brief summary of the course, intended only to convey its flavour by listing the title of each session, giving a word or two about each speaker and, in keeping with the theme of this book, a quotation from each which seemed at the heart of what they were saying and which, therefore, rang bells for me as well, I believe, as for the students.

---

[20] The Manager's Environment. Edited by Tony Giles, The Centre of Management in Agriculture and the Farm Management Unit, The University of Reading, 1990.

1. **Managing within the Environment in Practice**
   Presented by the previously quoted Andrew John, manager of Overbury Farms, Tewkesbury, who described his own farm management training and experience, indicating the breadth of the environmental network within which he did his job, wryly observing that:

   *'The closest politics, in its rawest sense, gets to this rural backwater is a heavy argument between John and Bill in the Star pub over a pint or two of local scrumpy late on a Saturday night, which, like the Council of Ministers in Brussels, will break off and start again the next day (or month) as soon as the doors are open.'*

2. **Professional Farm Management Associations**
   Presented by Philip James who, after a lifetime's experience in NAAS and ADAS, called heavily on his current dual role as Director of the Centre of Management in Agriculture (now the Institute of Agricultural Management) and Secretary of the International Farm Management Association to draw general lessons about the value of professional farm management associations, advising that:

   *'Exchanging news and opinions with others not only provides factual information and wisdom but also helps in the development of the individual himself.'*

3. **The Manager's Need for Training, Information and Advice**
   Presented by *Dr Len Norman*, Principal of Sparsholt College. Co-author of a standard farm management text, he used his extensive experience in agricultural education to demonstrate visually the myriad of training, information and advice that is available to farmers, cautioning that:

   *'Knowing which advice to accept and implement and which to reject is important ...... (and that) ...... in the final analysis farmers and farm managers must themselves make their decisions based upon the advice and information available to them – and live with the consequences of their decisions!'*

4. **Managers and Agribusiness**

   Presented by *Robin Wensley*. Now in partial retirement, he addressed the students whilst still the managing director of nearby BB and O Farmers following a career in various sectors of the agribusiness world – the structure of which he analysed in detail. To their amusement he spoke to the students as potential customers, warning them, simply but seriously, to:

   *'Be aware and beware!'*

5. **Managers and Society**
   Presented by *G E Jones*, agricultural economist turned rural sociologist, and member of the University's Department of Agricultural Extension and Rural Development for many years. Before his recent retirement, Gwyn Jones, as he is universally known (including by many in the advisory services), cast his net perhaps wider than any other speaker in emphasising the conflicts, contradictions and overlapping interests that exist for individuals in any society and in any sector of that society. The complexity of this situation, he suggested, means that:

   *'Each person is in a sense encapsulated within his society, being both **in** and **of** his society.'*

6. **Management and the Legal Environment**
   Presented by *Professor Bill Seabrooke* – professionally a Land Agent – initially from Reading's Department of Land Management but subsequently from the corresponding Department in the Portsmouth Polytechnic (now University). He described the foundations of British law and its application and relevance to a range of land-use and farming issues. Making no pretence of being a lawyer, Bill Seabrooke brought, with fascinating examples, just the right level of understanding to the course, emphasising that:

   *'Legal costs are high and often unpredictable ...... procedures can be extremely protracted ...... prudent managers should make themselves aware of the areas of law that their operations entail ...... to obtain a good idea of the legal implications before the event rather than after.'*

7. **Managing with the Natural Environment**
   Presented by *Eric Carter, CBE,* who, after a distinguished career in ADAS, became Adviser (then Consultant) to the Farming and Wild Life Advisory Group, tasks that he combined with a wide range of farming and countryside interests and responsibilities. Returning to his alma mater, he presented uniquely informed and balanced views to the course concerning the successful co-existence of farming and the natural environment, although, as he pointed out in salutary vein:

   *'There is nothing natural about farming ...... it is a delusion to think that returning to a make-believe past can solve the global crisis. In fact the danger we face is not of being too modern but rather of not being modern enough. For the first time we have the knowledge and means to create a paradise or a rubbish tip on earth. The choice is ours.'*

8. **Managers and the Economic Environment**
Presented by *Professor Tony Giles* – who felt he could not escape from being responsible for this session himself!

Pointing out that there is an economic aspect to virtually every topic, the speaker narrowed this wide subject down to four sub headings: the theoretical and practical relationship between economics and management; the impact of day-to-day economic influences, and the farming industry as part of the wider economy, in which context he reminded the class that:

> '*It has rightly been said that farming is not one of the sunset industries on which the sun will set because its product is no longer wanted.*'

9. **Managing within National and International Policies**
Presented by *Dr John Bowman*, now in partial retirement after a varied career which took him into industry, academia (Professor of Animal Production and Founding Director of the Centre for Agricultural Strategy at The University of Reading) and as Chief Executive of both the Natural Environment Research Council and the National Rivers Authority. With all the necessary insights to describe the inevitable complexities that accompany the formulation of any national and international policies, each year John Bowman used a topical and sensitive case study (eg the level of nitrates in ground water) to demonstrate the range and interaction of public and professional interests in such matters, destined, usually, to lead to compromise policies. Encouraging student participation, his 'networks of interest' regularly extended across three blackboards vividly demonstrating the difficulty of any farm manager trying to read the signals in order to help him make his decisions. Nevertheless, he said:

> '*The manager's need is to appreciate the mechanism of Government in a democratic society and the opportunity for individuals and organisations to express and further their views through communication and the ballot box. This involves much reading, listening and talking. It is a complex process of information gathering and is an essential aspect of the manager's responsibility to take account of the whole context on which the business is to be pursued.*'

10. **Managing in the Future**
Presented by *Professor Colin Spedding, CBE,* (more recently, Sir Colin), now retired after his illustrious university career, culminating as Reading's Pro Vice Chancellor, and one of the few retirees I know who really is busier than ever! Eminently equipped, following a lifetime's experience in agricultural research, teaching and administration, he

speculated about the future in his inimitable way, stressing the importance of genuinely thinking about it, pointing out – almost pleading – that:

> *'If things will not or cannot stay as they are, then we need to think, as intelligently as possible, about the way change may or will occur ...... (and) ...... flexibility should be retained ...... (because) ...... whatever changes we propose or encourage, we may get it wrong .... above all, therefore, we need an environment, including R & D, in which innovation will flourish ...... where new developments can be objectively explored and tested, without ridicule or extremist zeal.'*

In concluding here, I should stress again that the word 'environment' was used in the title of the course on which this chapter has been based, in the widest possible sense: *'everything that is not me'* as was once said. That does not mean that everything that is relevant was included: time and the existence of other courses dealing with aspects of the wider scene account for any omissions, whilst the breadth of what was included meant, inevitably (and desirably in my view) that there was some overlapping between sessions.

As previously noted, the student class contained a valuable mix, not only of undergraduates and postgraduates, but of those from home countries and from overseas. Not all of them would, by any means, have gone on into practical farming – but they would all (as I often reminded them) sooner or later be managing something – even if it was only themselves! Although much of the course had an agricultural slant, the word 'farm' was deliberately not included in the course title, and most of what was said was believed to be relevant to managers whatever their profession or industry. The aim was not to create 'experts' in everything that was talked about but, in a nutshell, to encourage those listening to *be aware and beware*'!

Incidentally, my favourite examination question for this class (relying on a poet this time, not a coach driver!) was:

> *'No man is an island, entire of itself'* (John Donne). Discuss this quotation in the context of managing a farm.

# 8 Cornerstones and Beliefs

I am conscious of the fact that, even in a book in which I deliberately set out to record what some of its practitioners have said to me about farm management, I have only scratched the surface of what I have heard and learned from them and from others: what I *took in* when acting as *'receiver'* and *passed* on to students and other farmers when acting as a *'transmitter'*.

Some of the pithier statements were passed on (as they have been here) more or less word for word, from 'receiver' to 'transmitter', put only into context by me. Much else that I have listened to has mingled with my own professional disciplines and attitudes to help form my personal approach to farm business management – whether I have been performing (often the right word!) in a classroom, conference hall, committee room, or out on the farm. In the process, I have come to recognise that, over the years, my approach has become based on a mixture of certain *cornerstones* and *beliefs*: the *cornerstones*, if you like, the individual tools of my trade and the *beliefs*, literally what I have come to believe about management – not least (but not only) when applied to farms. To the extent that it has been farmers and farm managers (and other professional colleagues) who have helped to point me in these various directions, it is only appropriate that those directions should form a chapter in this book.

Before embarking down that route, however, I should say that, when approaching any issue, I have always had a strong urge to first discover the facts: to find out what is happening, rather than what is thought to be happening, or might be happening because somebody thinks it is or believes that it should be. I cannot be sure whether this stems from my initial training as an economist or from some earlier and deeper curiosity about anything that has interested me. What I do know is that the early influence of Stuart Wragg, at Bristol, did nothing to discourage this attitude – which no doubt influenced the nature of my four cornerstones. It may also, incidentally, explain why I was prepared to remain as chairman of the national committee responsible for the Farm Management (later Business) Survey for almost twenty years. Within the limits of its brief, this Survey has always reflected exactly what is happening financially in British Agriculture and I have written about it in detail elsewhere[21]. Suffice to say here that measuring farming fortunes gave me more professional satisfaction than trying to forecast them. It was Galbraith who wrote that:

> *'The most common qualification of the economic forecaster is not in knowing, but in not knowing that he does not know'!*

---

[21] The Farm Business Survey: Its Origins, Development and Use (with D P Crawley) in Management Matters in 1991, FMU Study No 26, The University of Reading.

## CORNERSTONES

The dictionary defines cornerstones as an 'indispensable part or basis' – so it is the correct word to describe the principal tools in my personal business management kit. There are four of them; not, perhaps, especially unique, but certainly all very important to the job in hand. They are the *profit and loss account*, the *balance sheet, budgets,* and *budgetary control*. The first two have already been touched on in the financial section of my chapter on *What They Manage*, so I can discuss them briefly here and say a little more about the other two.

The profit and loss account is fundamental to knowing what is happening *now*. It has the merit (in this country) of being the one financial record that sooner or later has to be available (for statutory purposes) and, provided it is not too historic, is, therefore, a convenient basis for analysis. It is the responsibility of the management to decide how much more detail needs to be displayed for management purposes over and above what is needed by the Inland Revenue. This should not present accounting difficulties: you can't have a scrambled egg without first having had the egg! The other *great* merit of the profit and loss account is that it should, at least, tell the *whole* story and while the efficiency of individual enterprises and activities of course matters, it is their combination (there is usually more than one) into a whole business that generates a final single profit – the bottom line, which *does* matter. As I have said earlier on, I was always glad in my advisory days to be left alone for a short while with this summary of the whole financial situation (while others perhaps walked the farm) to discover what had been happening in the recent past – invariably the best guide there is to what is currently happening and what might well continue to happen in the immediate future. It is no accident, I believe, that in the majority of situations particular weaknesses and strengths persist year after year.

It is implicit in all that I have just written that the conventional layout of a profit and loss account – featuring as it does revenue, expenditure and opening and closing valuations – can be readily translated into meaningful statements of inputs and outputs, that, coupled with the necessary physical data, will permit the kind of orderly questioning and comparisons suggested in Figure 3 of Chapter 6. In my view, the rationale of these calculations has nowhere been better explained and illustrated than in the late Ford Sturrock's book on *Farm Accounting and Management*[22]. No doubt, these days, the necessary calculations are computerised, but I was personally happy, with or without a pocket calculator, to use my home-made flexible work sheet (Figure 5) to tell me most of what I wanted to know in order to lead discussion. That is why a profit and loss account has been the *first* of my cornerstones.

---

[22]Farm Accounting and Management. F G Sturrock, Pitman, London 1971.

# FIGURE 5 Output and Cost Calculation Form

## OUTPUT (£)

YEAR ENDING _____
HA _____

| | CATTLE | SHEEP | PIGS | POULTRY | MILK | CROPS | SUNDRIES |
|---|---|---|---|---|---|---|---|
| (1) RECEIPTS | | | | | | | |
| (2) CLOSING VALUATIONS | | | | | | | |
| (3) TOTAL (1) + (2) | | | | | | | |
| (4) PURCHASES | | | | | | | |
| (5) OPENING VALUATIONS | | | | | | | |
| (6) TOTAL (4) + (5) | | | | | | | |
| (7) OUTPUT (3) − (6) | | | | | | | |
| OUTPUT PER HA | | | | | | | |
| OUTPUT PER UNIT | | | | | | | |

### TOTAL OUTPUT

| ITEM | ACTUAL | PER HA |
|---|---|---|
| CATTLE | | − |
| SHEEP | | − |
| PIGS | | − |
| POULTRY | | − |
| MILK | | − |
| CROPS | | − |
| SUNDRIES | | − |
| TOTAL | | |

## COSTS (£)

| | BGHT. FOOD | BGHT. SEEDS | RENT & RATES | FERTI- LISERS | TOTAL LABOUR | POWER & MACH | SUNDRIES |
|---|---|---|---|---|---|---|---|
| (1) EXPENDITURE | | | | | | | |
| (2) OPENING VALUATIONS | | | | | | | |
| (3) TOTAL (1) + (2) | | | | | | | |
| (4) CLOSING VALUATIONS | | | | | | | |
| (5) COST (3) − (4) | | | | | | | |
| COST PER HA | | | | | | | |

### TOTAL COSTS

| ITEM | ACTUAL | PER HA |
|---|---|---|
| B'T FOOD | | |
| B'T SEEDS | | |
| FERTS | | |
| RENT | | |
| LABOUR | | |
| P. & M. | | |
| SUNDRIES | | |
| TOTAL | | |

| MARGIN | | |
|---|---|---|

My *second* cornerstone is the *balance sheet*. If the profit and loss account, coming along, as it does, year after year, resembles a moving picture, then the balance sheet is more like a periodic snapshot: a picture of the financial *base* from which annual trading emanates: and what is more important, in any situation, than a sound base? I have, in Chapter 6, already expressed the views that, provided the idiosyncrasies of accountancy jargon and layout can be unravelled, the important messages from the balance sheet need not be too many or too complex, with *Net Worth*, and what is governing it, taking pride of place. It is the first figure that a banker will turn to, and once the snapshot provided by the balance sheet is sufficiently clear and detailed he will (as the simplified layout below indicates) have all the evidence he needs about the financial scale, shape and status of any business in question:

Total Assets £ (being used)

less Total Liabilities £ (to others)

= Net Worth £ (owner's stake)

The relative strength of many farm balance sheets (ie their high net worth and correspondingly low gearing) has been referred to earlier, suggesting perhaps that, looking ahead, *asset management* could have an increasingly important part to play in the overall financial management of many farms. It is a phrase that was hardly heard in the not too distant past, but which may become more important in the future, if farming becomes faced with increasingly difficult trading prospects.

My *third* cornerstone has been to recognise the supreme importance of *budgeting* in all its various forms: traditional whole farm budgeting, partial budgeting, gross margins, and, more recently, net margins. The name given to whole-farm and partial budgeting makes their purpose self explanatory. In their different ways they each have a part to play in planning, decision-making and as a basis for exercising control. As a tool for exploring the possible outcome of marginal changes, partial budgets have been perhaps the most frequently used of all budgetary tools – more flexible in their use (embracing every item that will change) and safer than the simple comparison between gross margins which, in the hands of the unwary, can leave fixed costs dangerously out of the reckoning.

It is almost certain that the so-called fixed costs will change in magnitude and make-up as the scale of possible changes increases, perhaps to the point of scrapping or introducing whole enterprises. At that stage something more robust than either partial budgets or gross margins may be required and it is here that a renewed interest in net margins (akin but not identical to full costing) has been shown in recent years. I am again reminded here of my early days with Stuart Wragg and can picture now the glint in his eyes, when a farmer was imprudent enough to suggest getting out of something as basic to the success of his business as, say, milk production. With the skills of a surgeon, he would pick up the trading account, remove all milk and associated cattle sales, then all the allocatable costs (fixed as well as variable) and, pointing to the large 'hole' that was inevitably left in the account, ask,

> 'What are you going to do to fill that?!'

Much more recently, my discussions with farmers have led me to the conclusion that, as they search for radical ways and means of maintaining their profits, they have wanted to be reassured that each of their enterprises is pulling its weight: to be confident about its technical efficiency, to know how each is contributing to the overall profit, what call each is making on the 'pool' of fixed costs, and what would happen if a particular enterprise was significantly expanded, reduced or scrapped: precisely the kind of question that Wragg was posing.

With the days well and truly gone when most financial problems on most farms could be solved by simplistic marginal adjustments (usually involving expansion), an awareness of net margins will help to test the larger questions that, these days, have to be asked. In essence, this means taking gross margins a stage further, allocating to each enterprise *all* of those costs that can rationally be allocated to it. A few genuinely overhead costs never can be sensibly allocated. Like the telephone, they are there because the *business* is there not because this or that enterprise is. That is why it is appropriate to talk about the *net margin* and not the *profit* from each enterprise. The author has written in more detail about this elsewhere, from which Figure 6 is reproduced here to show how far both the gross and the net margins contribute towards final profit and how far, at the same time, each stops short of it[23].

None of this is to suggest that gross margins will not continue, along with other forms of budgeting, to have an important use in farm management analysis and planning – and where would we all be without John Nix's 'Pocket book' full of them! It is, rather, that there exists a range of budgeting tools and the nature of the problem will determine which one is the most appropriate one to use. As indicated, much will depend on the scale of any change that is being contemplated and which of the more fixed type of resources are in surplus or short supply at the time: what I have sometimes referred to as 'the jumping off point'.

My *fourth* and final cornerstone is budgetary control, for which my enthusiasm goes back long before the careful monitoring of individual enterprises became the vogue that it now is. It has always seemed to me that, as the simple layout below shows, the comparison of actual results with

---

[23] Net Margins and All That FMU Study No 9, The University of Reading, 1986.

# FIGURE 6 Contribution of Several Enterprises to Farm Profit via Gross and Net Margins

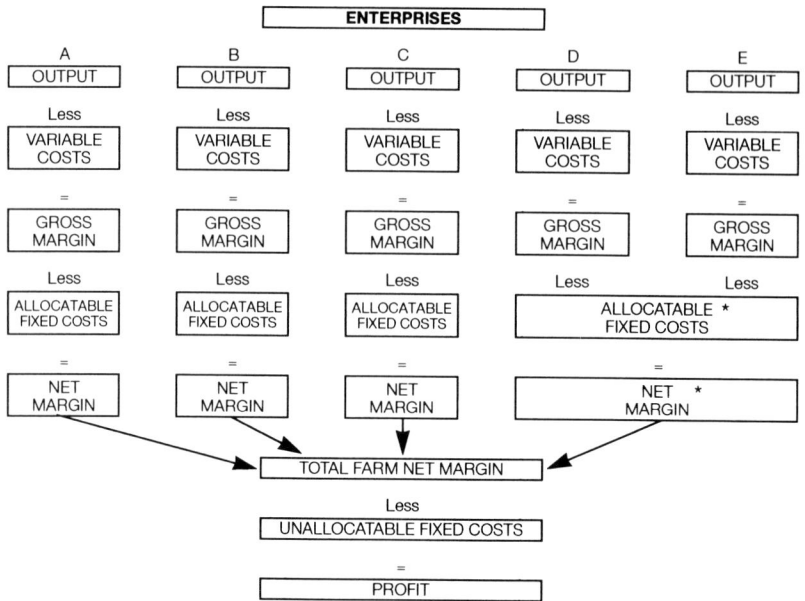

\* It may well be the case that a number of closely related enterprises (e.g. cereals) use the same specified fixed resources in which case a division of allocatable costs between them is not possible or helpful.

planned intentions is both conceptually and, in practice, such a fundamental matter as to be part and parcel of the whole philosophy of good management based on objectives and plans.

|  | No of cows | Yield per cow | Price per litre | Total |
|---|---|---|---|---|
| Planned Milk Production (p) | $N_p$ | $Y_p$ | $P_p$ | $£_p$ |
| Actual Milk Production (a) | $N_a$ | $Y_a$ | $P_a$ | $£_a$ |
| Difference | ? | ? | ? | ? |

The differences between any pair of items (eg $N_p$ and $N_a$), can be in either direction, above or below the plan, and some of the reasons for the differences will be quite outside the manager's control. That is unavoidable and does not invalidate the case for budgetary control, the purpose of which is to identify what *can* be controlled, to understand the reasons *why* there have been deviations from plans and, *where necessary* and *possible*, to take corrective action as *soon* as possible. Without *action* there is no control. In this sense budgetary control should be in tune with what farmers want most – to carry out the productive side of farming well and on time. I have always believed that, with the help of budgetary control, there is, in most farming situations, more scope for improving financial results (even in the mid-to-late 1990s) by tightening up on the performance of existing enterprises rather than by switching to alternatives, about which the farmer may know little or nothing. That is not to deny the need for radical change in some situations, but remember, as John Miller said:

> *'The best form of diversification is to do what you are already doing, better'*

**BELIEFS**
In the course of my involvement in the various tasks that I have described in this book teaching, advising, research and no small amount of management of university affairs – and as a result of my discussions along the way – I have developed a number of *beliefs* about management which are listed below. There are eight of them: none of them peculiar to farming – but all of them, I believe, relevant to farming.

*First*, the manager's job is characterised, ultimately, by its *totality*. In a farming context this means that it is not just about husbandry skills, or organising ability, and not even about the management of individual farm enterprises. It is about all of these things – and *anything* else that has to be managed – as individual farm enterprises become moulded into a single business. It is the *whole* business that has to be managed and it is, therefore, a comprehensive task which, depending upon the size and structure of the farm system, can be more or less complicated. As we have already noted, at the end of our consideration of *what they manage* in Chapter 6, the scope for delegating managerial responsibilities is usually very limited in farming, so that farmers are often the middle management and the senior management rolled into one. Even, however, on small farms, where a farmer may be under-employed in a strictly managerial (as opposed to manual) sense – which can often be the case – he (or she) will have to be managerially versatile. He may often, therefore, need advice and guidance from outside experts. Such help may never have been more important than it is as a new century beckons, with change and uncertainty being superimposed on the difficulties of recent years.

My second belief is that the nature of the farmer's job is not, in managerial terms, as different as may often be thought, from managing other kinds of business. After all, farmers are businessmen who are managing businesses that happen to be farms – and, with so much diversification, the definition of what constitutes a farm is, these days, getting more and more blurred.

Clearly the farm will have its own technical and husbandry features and problems, but so will most other businesses. And some of those other businesses will have problems, perhaps of staff management or marketing, which may not be present to the same degree on many farms. Many farmers and farm managers no doubt feel that they have more than their share of special problems – but, frankly, I doubt it, and, in terms of the principal managerial functions – setting objectives, planning, decision-making and controlling – they will have much in common with other types of managers – and much, therefore, to learn from each other. I have sometimes witnessed this at local meetings of the kind organised by the (British) Institute of Management where occasionally farmers mingle with their counterparts from other industries.

In this context, I have often argued that there is no such subject as farm management, only management applied to farms. I have been careful, however, where I have said this as my University would not want to have been seen to be funding a Chair in a non-existent subject! I have tried, therefore, to be strict about referring to my expertise as in *farm business management*, not simply *farm management*, in which, to my mind, the only experts are those who practise it – not those of us who write and talk about it!

*Thirdly*, I believe that, as with any businessman, what the individual farmer decides or tries to do with his business will reflect both the opportunities that the resources at his command permit (quantitatively and qualitatively) as well as his or her personal objectives. These two things – resources and objectives – will not usually be independent of each other: the one, rather, is likely to influence the other, in either or both directions. Furthermore, neither is likely to alter dramatically in the short term: the resources for financial reasons, and the objectives for more personal ones. I have, incidentally, never seen any mileage in those rather tedious arguments about whether farming is a business or a way of life. It is, always has been, and always will be, both – just like most other occupations. There will almost always be multiple objectives, often in conflict with each other, sometimes difficult to identify clearly and equally difficult to quantify precisely. They will often, therefore, be neglected for something easier and more pressing: like getting on with the day's work – and here, again, farmers will not be so different from other managers.

But, *fourth* on my list, I believe that shining through the haze of objectives there will be one that, sooner or later, in all circumstances, will emerge, crystal clear, as paramount. Quite simply, it will be the need to *survive*, preferably at whatever level is consistent with a required lifestyle: the *preferred future*. In the last analysis most, if not all, objectives will be secondary to this one – and, over time, some appropriate level of profits will be necessary to permit that survival. This does not necessarily mean maximising profits in some economic textbook sense: indeed, Drucker often talks about businessmen looking for the *minimum* level of profit that they require to satisfy their needs. But, to use the economists jargon, that minimum will come high on any list of 'satisficers'. I should stress, however, that this view should not imply any lack of awareness for other, non-financial, satisficers, or for wider responsibilities to society and accepted codes of managerial behaviour. My one-time colleague and cricketing companion, Graham Dalton, long since based in Aberdeen, came close to the nub of all this when he said that:

> *'The acid test of any manager is integrity in the husbandry of all his resources, including land and the wild life, the care of his workforce and concern for his customers'*

*Fifthly*, I believe that it is impossible to teach anyone to be a manager. What *can* be taught is an understanding of what the subject is about, how to use particular techniques and an awareness of ways of thinking that may help. A long time ago I gave up any belief that I could teach farmers in any formal sense – and certainly not provide them with answers: remember the coach driver's *'trial and error'!* What I *could* perhaps offer was how, as an economist, I thought about *their* situations and problems, in a way that might be helpful to them. And in situations where the audience could talk to each other, as well as listen to the speaker, I had no doubt that perhaps their greatest benefits were in recognising the similarity of each other's problems and having an opportunity to discuss them with each other – away from the farm, with the lecturer as catalyst.

I should add here that what I have just written about teaching management to farmers (or, rather, *not* teaching them) is, in my opinion, even more true for students. They can, of course, be taught *about* management but they cannot be taught to *be* managers and, contrary to the views of some of their elders, they are the first to acknowledge that. They know that after theory comes practice and experience and that there is no short cut to managerial competence.

Mention of competence leads me to my *sixth* belief, namely that management training is about training managers to be good and better at their job, not necessarily to become super-managers. As farmer and consultant, and personal friend, Gordon Lugg, has said:

> *'A training in farm management is a training for life'*

and most of us, in whatever we do in life, are not too far away from the average. We should not expect others to be different. In any situation, doing a few of the most important things well is a more realistic objective than trying to be expert in everything, especially in an industry like farming, calling, as we have seen, for such a diverse range of skills. Farmers, like other managers, should not be handicapped by feeling the need to do everything that has to be done in their businesses. Others, inside and outside the business are there to help provide breadth and depth of skills and knowledge. The manager's job is to hold it all together and, increasingly, with the help of Information Technology, he will need to know where information and knowledge is, rather than to carry it around with him. And what will be increasingly important in such circumstances will be the need to be selective in where reliable information is sought, whilst retaining independent judgement in how to use it.

This leads me directly to my *seventh* belief. Those of us who are at the 'transmitting' end of information and ideas, owe it to those on the 'receiving' end to be conscious of our responsibilities and, in the first instance at least, to learn to keep our 'message' as clear as we can. When so-called 'experts' talk to general practitioners they will, in the nature of things, usually be talking about issues and complexities that are their daily professional concern. In these circumstances, the over-use of jargon and complicated techniques (from which management specialists are not immune!) can build barriers to understanding rather than remove them. There is nothing condescending in what I am saying. Specialists quickly become non-specialist as soon as they move out of their own fields – and are then themselves grateful to those who can keep things simple. There is time enough in most situations for details and complexities to be added after initial understandings have been soundly achieved.

Trying to practise what I have preached, on this score, I have made a habit of approaching various aspects of management with the help of some fairly simple diagrams (like the four 'boxes' for financial management) in order to get me (the transmitter) and my audience (the receivers) on to the same wavelength. As a further example, I have found it helpful when discussing farm planning, to do so with the help of Figure 7 below, with the suggestion that (short of getting out of it) there are, in any situation, only four ways to improvement:

1) Increasing gross margins.

2) Changing the system.

3) Reducing fixed costs.

4) Adding something.

Farm planning, I know, is not exactly as simple as that. There is usually a wide variety of further options within each of these four. But I believe it is helpful, in the first instance, to have a clear view of the strategic options, as set out in the diagram, before allowing detail and complexities to complicate the picture.

# FIGURE 7 A Systematic Exploration of Profit Increasing Options

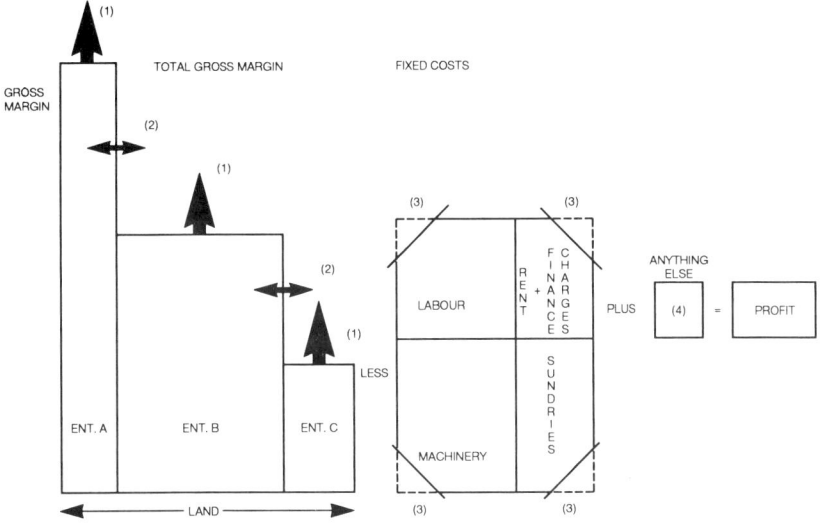

In concluding this chapter, I should say that I first set down my management beliefs when giving my valedictory lecture – the Edith Mary Gayton Memorial Lecture – at Reading in the Autumn of 1992. Since then I have reflected on them on various occasions, wondering, in particular, if I needed to reduce them or add to them. In the event I have decided to do neither. There are still, therefore, *eight*, and *only* eight of them, and I come now to the last. It is quite simply the need, in the light of various references here to long term objectives and strategies, to stress the importance, also, of day-to-day tactical decisions: the attention to detail and the importance of managing well *now*. A pre-condition of long term survival is survival each day and each year as they come along. It would be totally counter-productive if too much preoccupation with the future resulted in a neglect of the present – perhaps to the point that there is no future. I have seen it happen. But observation over the years has told me that the best and most successful managers have thought carefully about both strategy and tactics. They are doing the right things (for the future) and are doing them well (in the present). The big things *and* the little things matter. It is part and parcel of the totality of management (my *first* belief). Getting it *all* right is a daunting task. But it is what good management is about.

# 9 Just Like Christmas

## AN ACADEMIC RETIREMENT

I return, in part, in this penultimate chapter to my autobiographical threads – and in particular to retirement. Forty years of being a professional agricultural economist came to an end on the last day of September, 1993, and I woke up the next morning feeling glad to have got there more or less unscathed: a feeling that I now know is shared by others, despite any outward appearances of self confidence.

I suppose that, in a sense, I continued to be, and still am, an agricultural economist – but on that October morning a pension replaced a salary, and I felt the luxury of being able to decide, day-by-day, what I wanted to do. I immediately discovered that, henceforth, the *weather* would prove to be a far more important factor in this than ever before: no great point in setting off for Lords or the Oval under threatening skies, with the freedom – denied in employment – to wait for the sun. But my wife, Heather, and I *did* set off on that first 'free' day for a welcome weekend, near Chichester. Heather's teaching commitments meant that the Grand Tour had to wait until the next summer, but some immediate space seemed like a priority.

Sooner or later, of course, everybody has to retire. For those in paid employment somebody else will normally decide 'when', whilst, for the self-employed, it will be a matter of choice, governed usually by personal and domestic considerations. What is common to most of us, however, is the knowledge that some form of retirement is inevitable, and that, as it approaches, it will be sensible to make some preparations for the adjustments that lie ahead. This may not always be easy, especially for those who have not tempered professional or business careers with other interests or hobbies, and who have to face the termination of their occupation on a particular day: a day that, with or without preparation, will arrive – quite suddenly – just like Christmas!

In my own case I found it helpful – and would counsel others accordingly – to distinguish clearly between *retiring* and *retirement*. Retiring comes at a particular *point of time*, whilst retirement is a *phase* of life – the next occupation – which needs to be *prepared* for and *lived,* and the more the former can be subsumed into the latter the better.

I do not underestimate my own good fortune in this respect. Not the least civilised part of university life is the opportunity to begin the preparation for retirement at a sensible time, so as to permit what my long-standing colleague and then Head of Department, John Marsh, referred to as a 'planned exit'. If it sounded a bit like euthanasia I don't think it was intended to, and, not wanting to spend too much of my final years focusing on *not being there*, I began preparing for my 'exit' about two years before departure. In the event, this proved to be about the right time span, allowing me to relinquish various administrative jobs and committee posts both in the University and outside. In several cases I was able to help choose and train my successor, which was satisfying. It also happened that, at the time, degree courses in Reading's Faculty of Agriculture and Food were being re-vamped to fit 'modularisation', so it was sensible for me to hand over most of my teaching to those who would be around to teach. I hung on, however, to the bitter end, to farm classes (and, therefore, my contact with farmers) and to my course on *The Manager's Environment*, together with a small amount of external examining which would automatically come to an end as its three year appointments ran out.

I, therefore, embarked on my final year in the University with a fairly clean sheet, able to concentrate on clearing my room – a mammoth task after forty years of accumulating paper and the part of my job that I enjoyed most – writing. I was anxious, while still in harness, with full access to secretarial help, to make good progress with a number of reflective studies some of which would be published before I retired – notably *Windows on Agricultural Economics and Farm Management* (an anthology of my writings about the history of my subject), and others, like *See You at Oxford* (a history of the Oxford Farming Conference on its fiftieth anniversary) with some of the spade-work done, to be completed afterwards.

In this way, my final years in employment blended with my early years out of it – especially as, for many years, most of my writing had been done at home. One day a week, at least, had been given over to this activity – necessarily away from the interruptions of telephones, colleagues and students. These were *appointments with myself* – as I have always called them – of sufficient duration to allow progress: part and parcel of my belief in the importance of time management. Farmers please take note. I have never forgotten the Berkshire dairy farmer, Tony Wood, who completed large tracts of a time-sheet he was keeping for me, as part of a survey, with the letters B.A.G. When asked what this meant he said:

'Buggering about in general'!

I often wondered if he was the most honest farmer in the survey!

So now my personal situation has simply gone into reverse, with most of the week spent at home and one day a week, in my Emeritus capacity, in the University, to *enjoy* telephones, colleagues and students! And if I spend most of my time indulging the pleasure I derive from writing, it is interspersed by working on my garden and allotment (where Malcolm Stansfield says I am at last learning something about soil chemistry!), watching cricket and rugby, live and on screen, having time for numerous other interests, and keeping generally in touch with the world of farm management. In this respect, chairing the Organising Committee for the Tenth Congress of the International Farm Management Association, held at Reading University in 1995, and helping to fashion the Institute of Agricultural Management out of the CMA – with all of the farming contacts that both activities provided – have given particular satisfaction.

In these various ways, therefore, the moment of *retiring* became part and parcel of the longer term *job of retirement*, minimising any sense of withdrawal symptoms. I knew from past experience that I seldom missed anything that I had to give up, providing there was something else to move on to. In this case, the next job has been retirement, and after forty years as a paid agricultural economist – most of which I enjoyed – it was actually nice to stop.

## FARMING RETIREMENT

As already indicated, I am conscious of my own good fortune in all this; how, *not in my wildest dreams*, I was somehow led down the route of agricultural economics and farm management, into University employment with the freedoms of interest that (even these days) it allows. I appreciate that not all occupations provide comparable opportunities for phasing employment into retirement – although, as it happens (and research findings confirm), farming, especially for the self-employed, is amongst those that are most likely to. This view was confirmed in two reports published by Reading's Farm Management Unit in 1990 and 1991. They were jointly entitled *Getting Out of Farming?*, one dealing with the position of farm managers and the other with self employed farmers.

The precise origins of many research projects are often difficult to trace and whatever the method of origin it is invariably difficult to pinpoint them in time. More often than not, however, one piece of work or contact leads to another, as was the case in this instance – the details of which may be of interest. For a good many years I had been inviting Pat Oakley, the Agricultural Manager of Lloyds Bank, to give a lecture, from the standpoint of a banker, to an undergraduate course on financial management. The friendship which followed found us sitting together at a dinner at the Oxford Farming Conference of 1985, when Pat enquired about the prospects for graduates getting an entrée into farming without a family farm to start in. As a direct result of that conversation it was decided to launch a study of the problems faced by graduates in the situation envisaged, and three years later, with help from Lloyds Bank and Pat Oakley himself, a report on *Non-inherited Business 'Start-up's* was published[24]. Summarising the

---

[24] Getting Started in Farming. A Study of Non-inherited Business 'Start-ups'. A J Errington, A K Giles and PC Oakley, FMU Study No 15, The University of Reading 1988.

experiences of 55 young people in the Reading Province who had got started in farming without the benefits of a family farm, the report concluded that, despite the obvious capital problems, the obstacle can, 'with hard work, help and perseverance be overcome'. And there the matter might have stopped, if one thing had, once again, not led to another. In this case, it was when ex-farm manager turned consultant, Nigel Agar, happened to read the *Getting Started* report. A good friend of this writer – then and now – Nigel, still fresh from the trauma of getting *out* of farming while in mid career, telephoned me from his home in Cambridgeshire just to say:

> '*Getting started in farming isn't the major problem – it's getting out – and that's what your next study should be about.*'

In accepting this challenge, my colleague and co-author, Andrew Errington, and I, recognised that here, at least, if not in their day-to-day work, there was a major difference in the circumstances of the salaried farm manager and the self employed farmer, and that any study should encompass both groups. We decided, therefore, to sub-divide the task and with different samples and questionnaires, this meant, in effect, two separate studies, leading eventually to the *'Getting Out'* reports previously referred to: Part I, dealing with farm managers, to be written by myself and Part II, dealing with farmers, by Andrew[25]. In the event, Andrew collaborated with Richard Tranter from Reading's Centre for Agricultural Strategy, and Part II took on the substantially wider brief of 'short term adjustment and plans for long term change in English farm family businesses'.

On the specific question of retirement, however, Errington and Tranter ascertained from a national sample of over eight hundred farmers that intentions were varied. Thirty four percent of respondents expected to retire *eventually* (whatever that might mean!), 53% expected to *semi-retire* and 13% said that they would *never* retire from farming. Nearly two-thirds had got as far as seriously discussing their retirement (sometimes with accountants, solicitors or bank managers) especially where sons and daughters existed. Three quarters of the sample were already contributing to a private pension scheme, with the expectation that other sources of retirement income would include, in addition to state pensions, the sale of farm assets and, in the case of those contemplating semi-retirement, a continuing share of farm profits. Even, however, amongst the total 87% expecting to retire or to semi-retire, there seemed likely to be varying

---

[25] Getting Out of Farming?
Part One: Farm Managers. A K Giles, FMU Study No 25, The University of Reading, 1990.
Part Two: The Farmers. Andrew Errington and Richard Tranter, FMU Study No 27, The University of Reading, 1991.

degrees of physical mobility, with no more than 60% of them expecting to move out of their existing houses – presumably the farmhouses.

This analysis suggests that for most self-employed farmers retirement is likely to be ill-defined in terms of time and age, and that many of them will be in the happy position of being able to phase retirement over a period of time rather than having to confront it at some specific point of time: and certainly not to have it determined by someone else. The reality of this situation is that their eventual role, even in what is described as 'some form of retirement', could vary from that of being the 'gaffer' who still signs all the cheques and, therefore, governs the major decisions, to being the person who is most expendable and is therefore usefully employed as 'the boy', to run errands when things break down. The author has seen both extremes in action, and everything in between. He has met only a few farmers who, before age has overtaken them, have either sold up or stepped sideways into something recognisable as orthodox retirement, leaving opportunities to younger members of the family.

Farm managers are obviously in a much more cut and dried position, all knowing that whether they or their employers make the decision, retirement will almost certainly come at some specific time and will usually mean an end to the job they have been doing. The picture that emerged from Part One of *Getting Out of Farming*, (largely confirmed by the CMA's surveys of *Farm Managers' Salaries*), is that the majority of farm managers, mostly with little or no experience of other occupations, hope to remain in farming until they cease full-time employment. They have embarked on salaried farm management because farming has been their first love, and, in the absence of sufficient capital, could only farm in the way that they have. Relatively few of them have significant income from other sources and once established in farm management the majority prefer not to leave until they have reached the milestone in age of either 60 or 65. A high proportion have a pension scheme with their jobs and an even higher proportion of those without such a scheme make private provision. Nearly three-quarters of them own a house.

It is of interest that of the small proportion (11%) of this sample who did not expect to remain in farming until they retired, *all* had professional qualifications, *all* owned a house and *all* had private pension arrangements. With their ages ranging between 27 and 53, their intentions, without exception, were to leave sooner rather than later.

The wisdom of this intention was, incidentally, born out by the stories of seven ex-farm managers who were not part of the main survey but whose experiences, having already left the industry, were included in the report as separate case-studies. Their stories tended to confirm Nigel Agar's assertion that getting out of farming before retirement is a major problem.

Nevertheless, threatened by the notorious insecurity of the job, they had taken the plunge. There was a common thread to their separate stories which, to a greater or lesser extent, pointed to the importance of the following factors:

- luck
- not waiting too long
- some business experience
- personal contacts
- some prior knowledge of a chosen alternative
- no heavy capital requirements
- not expecting the perfect alternative immediately
- a supportive wife
- privately owned accommodation
- the need to balance income with security
- keeping physically and mentally alert

and, in the context of this chapter:

- planning for retirement.

At the time, I observed that these *common threads* might well provide helpful guidelines for any manager changing any job: yet another example of the similarity, rather than the differences, between farming and other industries.

What we have seen in the latter part of this Chapter is a glimpse of the circumstances of two sets of people, to all intents and purposes doing very similar jobs, but from different financial and employment situations: the one group with their capital and profits at risk, and the other with their jobs and salaries at risk. For the former group it is clear their retirement is likely to be far less cut and dried than it will be for the latter. But it was clear from the studies referred to here, that what they will have in common when they retire is a similar attitude to what they will and what they will not miss. What they will both miss will primarily be about the nature of the job itself – working with crops and livestock, living in the countryside and (even the managers) enjoying a high degree of independence. What both groups will be most glad to be away from is little to do with the job itself, but rather some general indefinable combination of irritations and what both groups referred to as *'hassle'* – something with which most of us are familiar!

# 10 Stocktaking

The early stages of retirement seem to generate a curiosity on the part of others as to how one is coping: a curiosity that sometimes carries with it an element of surprise - or is it disappointment? – that the answer may be "very well, thank you"! Certainly one has to field some standard and oft repeated questions, the most common of which is:

*'I expect you are busier than ever?'*

In most cases (but not all) I have managed not to say that I have felt mildly insulted by the question – but sometimes I have been unable to resist pointing out that I believed I worked hard whilst I was employed and in no way could I be, or am I, 'busier than ever'! Occupied, yes, but doing only what I want to, when I want to – with any 'working day' now lasting only from about 10 am to 4 pm (instead of 8 until 6!) with evenings and weekends free to relax. And what I do during the main part of each day is governed by the weather and whatever of my various personal interests happen to be competing for my time.

So 'no', in no way am I busier than ever, and 'no', I do not miss doing what I did for forty years – which is surely enough of any job! I hope that I am tactful about how I say the second 'no', not wanting previously close friends and colleagues to feel offended – but I am, of course, fortunate that my situation enables me to continue friendships and those professional interests – some of them fairly menial – which still appeal to me: a bit, I have sometimes thought, like being a semi-retired farmer and acting as 'the boy' !

But the comment that I most relish comes more in the form of a statement than a question:

*'It's important that you keep your mind active'.*

This, I know (like the other questions) is well intentioned – so I gently, but firmly, point out that it is my *body*, not my *mind* that I am worried about! As far as I can tell, my mind did not stop functioning normally on the day that I ceased to be an active academic – and, short of some medical disaster, nor, I believe, is it likely to. On the contrary, looking back on *some* of the things that I had to cope with in recent years – as administrative chores and paper work multiplied in response to increased financial constraints (*'the cost of keeping costs down is going up all the time'*) – I am inclined to think that I have had more time since retirement, not less, to *think* properly.

By contrast, my body constantly reminds me of advancing years. I am already a fully fledged member of the 'prostate club', while early injuries incurred in the service of other clubs – notably rugby and cricket – increasingly come home to roost. I like to think that I am not, by nature, a hypochondriac – but I am doing whatever I can – without I hope, *becoming one* – to keep my body active, while the mind looks after itself!

Colin Spedding has often reminded us that he finds it easier now to think about the past than the future – *'because there is more of it to think about'*. And certainly much of my own thinking since retirement has been of a reflective kind. It has been a time for personal as well as professional stocktaking. Twice before in recent years I have, anticipating retirement no doubt, had occasion to compile a brief professional stocktaking: once for my Presidential Address to the Agricultural Economics Society, in 1987, and secondly for my valedictory Edith Mary Gayton Memorial Lecture in 1992. The first was seen principally through the eyes of an agricultural economist and the second, wearing my farm management hat. To the extent, however, that the former embraces the latter, it seemed appropriate that I should combine the two in the final chapter of this book: a list, if you like, of the assets I have enjoyed in my professional *balance sheet*: assets that perhaps others working in the same broad arena of agricultural economics and farm management might recognise – and share.

First, I have been fortunate in being able to combine my early and instinctive interest in the physical fashioning of the landscape and the human impact upon it with a subsequent interest in management – an empirical arm of economics. In the process this has provided a link with land and the countryside which seems to satisfy some basic need in more than mere agricultural economists!

Secondly, to the extent that agricultural economics in its widest sense, and farm management in particular, are directly or indirectly concerned with some part of the food chain and the amenity provision of the countryside, there is the satisfaction for those of us involved of being concerned not with the trivial or ephemeral, but with a basic and universal requirement of mankind.

Thirdly, there has been the wider satisfaction of being involved in an applied discipline which interacts with many others: pure and applied, scientific and social. In this way the 'cocktail' of farm management, as a subject, reflects the *totality* that I have ascribed earlier on to practical farm management.

Fourthly, it follows from the previous paragraph that I have had the pleasure and support of working with others. Few agricultural economists or farm management specialists work alone.

We experience none of the intellectual and physical loneliness of some occupations, including, to some extent, farming. Quite apart from close academic and supporting colleagues, there have been constant opportunities to meet, work with, and make lasting friendships with academics from elsewhere, civil servants, those in professions and commerce, and especially, of course, farmers, farm managers and their employees and families[26].

Fifthly, my work has provided the opportunities for travel, not only throughout the United Kingdom, appreciating its unrivalled variations and beauty – but elsewhere in Europe and around the world. Between 1964 and 1985, triennial meetings of the International Association of Agricultural Economists took me successively to Lyon, Sydney, Minsk, Sao Paolo, Nairobi, Banff, Jakarta and Malaga. Between its first meeting at Warwick and its tenth at Reading, I attended four of the International Farm Management Association's biennial Congresses – at Guelph, Copenhagen, Palmerston North and Christchurch in New Zealand, and Budapest. In addition, lecturing and consultancy has taken me into various parts of Belgium, France, Turkey, Poland and South Africa.

An important by-product of this travel has been the understandings that have been developed and the friendships, often stretching over many years, that have been cemented: not only with other nationals but often with fellow countrymen and even close colleagues with whom the normal round of work often precludes relaxed conversation. There have been too many of them to mention by name but I hope they will know who they are.

As I have said in an earlier chapter, the opportunity to see much of overseas farming on these visits is often limited, confined at most to a day or two out during or after a conference. On those few occasions, however, I have seen and heard enough from host farmers to understand what it means to be farming in situations as diverse as the North American corn belt, the coffee plantations in Brazil, collective farms in Eastern Europe, sheep stations in

---

[26] In addition to the various colleagues, farmers and farm managers who have already been mentioned in the text, any record of those with whom I have worked closely and enjoyed friendship would be incomplete without mention, also, of Reading colleague David Ansell (a frequent co-author, fellow traveller and cricketing companion)and, more latterly, Andrew Errington who assisted, and then took over from me, in various aspects of management before departing, as I write, for a new Chair at Seale Hayne. And 'lodged' in Reading has been Philip James, with whom I have worked closely in recent years under the CMA (now the I.Agr.M.) and IFMA umbrellas. In Whitehall there was a sequence of MAFF economists, including Joe Evans, Sheila Dickinson and Peter Muriel, who 'kept house' for the FBS while I chaired its national committee – aided and abetted by Manchester University's incomparable (and incorrigible!) Bill Richardson, who chaired the important Methodology Working Party. An equally close friend with whom I shared examining and tutoring during his Seale Hayne days was Mike Atkinson. Mention of individuals in this way, is, I know, invidious; but all of these stand alongside those already mentioned, and many more whom space does not permit a mention, but who are not forgotten – as respected colleagues, associates and intimates, with whom, over forty years, I have shared laughter as well as work.

Australia, dairying in New Zealand, tea plantations in Kenya and Indonesia, vineyards in South Africa – and many more. And it has convinced me that managers have much in common with each other between countries – just as they do between industries.

Sixth on my list of 'assets', I am grateful that my job has given me the opportunity to - indeed demanded that I should – write. This is not always easy, as one struggles to be precise in the often imprecise area of management. I can nevertheless look back on nearly two hundred publications as a labour of love, satisfying, I suspect, some creative urge: akin, perhaps, to the satisfaction that farmers derive from watching crops and livestock grow.

Mention of watching things grow points to another, seventh, asset: that of seeing young students mature and move successfully into jobs: constantly better equipped and in many ways more mature than the generation that has taught them. I have already paid tribute to their lack of arrogance – and have never underestimated the value of being in close contact with young people with alert and critical minds. That said, I must also say how much personal satisfaction I have gained from lecturing to postgraduates and speaking to farming audiences, both of which groups, in the nature of things, have more experience and awareness of farming and managerial realities than undergraduates can have. In many ways it has been the farmers who have been most helpful in reflecting back to me their approval or not of my views.

My eighth and final asset has, quite simply, been the privilege of having spent my working life (apart from National Service) in a University. I enjoyed Bristol but, in terms of years alone, Reading has dominated. For a few years, I was close to the cloistered elegance of its London Road site, before moving to one of Britain's most attractive campuses in Whiteknights. Despite expansion and constraints, the University of Reading has retained its friendly and civilised working atmosphere, with plenty of opportunity to meet those other than agriculturists. But perhaps because of their close contact with the industry they help to serve, my two Departments (Agriculture, and Agricultural Economics and Management), have had a special flavour about them which they should guard jealously. No ivory tower, Reading has been too near the centre of things, agriculturally and otherwise, for me to have ever seriously wanted to move.

If these then, have been my personal professional assets, there have, no doubt, been some liabilities to set against them. It would be misleading and untruthful to pretend that it has *all* been straightforward; and even more so to say that it has *all* been enjoyable. Life in any sphere is not like that and cannot be. As the list of assets suggests, however, a very large proportion of it *has* been – and has been rewarding. I am in no doubt that the assets have far outweighed the liabilities and that the balance sheet has, therefore, been strong; just like that of most farms!

# Postscript

I am learning from experience that I have become incapable of writing a book without adding a postscript. I am not sure why this is so, but there could be several reasons. Perhaps, as many authors admit, there is a reluctance to reach the point where the completed manuscript ceases to be 'theirs' and is shortly to become public property, with some inevitable loss of interest. Or perhaps, it is simply a reluctance to put the pen down (in my case it *still* is a pen!), rather as one is reluctant to come to the last page of a book one has enjoyed reading.

Most of my previous postscripts have been in books about professional organisations or sporting clubs and have had in common the fact that I have wanted, before coming to an end, to stress that the institutions in question depend for their importance on the people, of whom, individually and collectively, they are composed.

I suspect that I am having the same sort of feeling now, as I find myself writing this particular Postscript: that *farm management*, as a job or profession, depends for its importance on the character and ability of those who perform it: and they should not, individually or collectively, be lost sight of in any discussion of the subject.

One of the main purposes of this book has, of course, been to recall and quote some of the farmers and farm managers I have known: *the managers as farmers*. But I am conscious of the fact that I have, inevitably, only scratched the surface of the many others I have known, listened to and learned from: virtually all of those with whom I have conversed in any measure. They have all, as well as those whom I have quoted, contributed to my '*beliefs*' – and I hope they will know that.

I suppose that collectively farmers are no more (certainly no less) attractive than any other homogeneous group of professionals, but few would deny the existence of a camaraderie in the agricultural world that is easy to recognise and to enjoy. It embraces not only the farming community itself but those in the *ancillary* or *service* occupations many (but not all) of whom have themselves had agricultural backgrounds or training. Those of us who have come in from outside farming (like this writer), feel privileged to belong to this particular 'club' which seems to transcend both local and national boundaries.

Perhaps more than anywhere else in *this* nation, this spirit of camaraderie is present and visibly demonstrated at the annual Oxford Farming Conferences. Despite many necessary changes and developments in recent years, its spirit and traditions owe much, still, to the influence of its long-serving Secretary Mike Soper (1952 to 1980) — another of those from whom I have learned and whose friendship I have valued. Trying to catch the flavour of this prestigious Conference, I wrote in my recent account of its history that:

> 'It is important for organisers to take into account that delegates attend with a variety and mixture of objectives: to listen to well-known speakers, to learn, to recharge batteries, to socialise, to have fun, to make contacts and to be made alert to the issues of the day which may affect their farming or other professional work. Some devotees, young and old, have told the author that continuing attendance at Oxford over the years has been like an extension to, and in some cases a substitute for, college or university. The Conference should be structured — but not too structured — in order to permit these various objectives to be met.'

This summary of what makes Oxford 'tick' is perhaps at the heart also of the wider farming 'club'. That club, however, has no membership form, no subscription as such, and no written rules. It just exists. And, as its members know, there are 'little Oxfords' being held for them, day in and day out, up and down the country. Long may that wider club flourish.

## ADDENDUM

At the time that this book was going to print, his many friends and admirers heard the sad news of Peter Cockburn's premature death. He has been quoted several times in my text and although he was unable to read it, I had, when visiting him during his last days, shown him the cover on which he appears in very typical pose and being listened to. I think he was pleased and so was I. As a highly respected colleague and close friend he was, indeed, *a manager as farmer whom 'I have known'*.

> *A little while, a little while*
> *the land is ours a little while,*
> *and then we go we know not where*
> *and England is our children's care.*
>
> Clemence Dane